Fixing Legal
Injustice
in America

For my uncle Elliot "Beau" Lyon

Fixing Legal Injustice in America

The Case for a Defender General of the United States

Andrea D. Lyon

ROWMAN & LITTLEFIELD
Lanham • Boulder • New York • London

Published by Rowman & Littlefield
An imprint of The Rowman & Littlefield Publishing Group, Inc.
4501 Forbes Boulevard, Suite 200, Lanham, Maryland 20706
www.rowman.com

86-90 Paul Street, London EC2A 4NE, United Kingdom

British Library Cataloguing in Publication Information Available

Library of Congress Cataloging-in-Publication Data Available

ISBN 9781538164655 (cloth: alk. paper) | ISBN 9781538164662 (electronic)

Contents

Foreword

Cynthia W. Roseberry

In the absence of competent defense counsel, justice is "but a fleeting illusion to be pursued, but never attained."[1] This truth is ingrained in the Sixth Amendment to the United States Constitution and recognized in common law in *Gideon v. Wainwright*.[2] Confidence in the criminal legal system is undergirded by justice. Justice demands equality. The "noble ideal," as Justice Hugo Black wrote in *Gideon*, of "fair trials before impartial tribunals in which every defendant stands equal before the law . . . cannot be realized if the poor man charged with crime has to face his accusers without a lawyer to assist him."[3]

When one considers the broad discretionary power of prosecutors in the criminal legal system, the gauntlet flung at the defense creates a veritable David-and-Goliath confrontation. The prosecutor has access to resources that exponentially outweigh those of indigent people accused of a crime. The power of the government has a coercive effect in plea negotiations; as a result, a majority of indigent people accused of a crime waive the right to a trial and accept a plea.

Nevertheless, indigent people appear in courtrooms across the United States to answer accusations alone, without competent defense counsel. I have personally witnessed an indifference to upholding the right to competent defense counsel. The despair in the pleas of the accused is not enough, it seems, to encourage examination of the facts through the lens of constitutional and common law. What results is an illusion of justice without substance.

Weaving narrative from the real people affected by the criminal legal system, Andrea Lyon makes the case for a Defender General. Too many real people face the possibility of imprisonment without a competent defense lawyer. The ability to afford a lawyer should not determine the amount of justice a person deserves.

While the issue of funding for a defense alone is sufficient to support the call for a Defender General, the other reasons pointed out in this book are equally important: specifically, the ability to influence policy. Our nation's federal public defenders expertly provide advocacy in the courtroom and on Capitol Hill, but across our nation, in the smallest places where the light of national media does not shine, public defenders need a seat at the policy table.

Sure, there are issues that need to be worked out, like the tension between the duty to defend the client at hand and the call to change the system writ large. Unlike prosecutors, defense lawyers cannot take a single call and apply it to every client. So, for example, if there were a call to deny every plea agreement and to take every case to trial, while the system would lose the power of coercive pleas that infringe on the right to a trial, the individual client would not be served in the case where a plea is in the client's best interest.

The current systems do not equally serve indigent people charged with crimes. Across America the systems are underfunded, not independent from the judiciary, and inconsistent in structure and execution.[4] America deserves more than an illusion of justice. We need to fortify the public defender system in our nation, and the creation of a Defender General of the United States is urgently needed.

Acknowledgments

I would like to thank the Alliance for a Defender General for their ideas and support of this project and this book. I also thank, with profound gratitude, E. Kate Cohn, my colleague who was an integral part of this book.

Some early readers/advisers also helped a great deal: Raymond Brown, Geoff Burkhart, Evan Griffith, Christine Filip, Sara Kadoura, Ernie Lewis, Elliot Lyon, Cynthia Roseberry, Tony Thedford, Kyleen Tremont, and the amazing Emily Hughes.

Thanks to my agent, Regina Ryan, and Becca Beurer of Rowman & Littlefield for their belief in this project.

Finally, I am profoundly grateful to my sisters and brothers who fight this good fight and my clients who have taught me so much.

Introduction

When I was in the Chicago public defender's office and assigned to a felony courtroom, I had a remarkably interesting client—sort of.

The Sixth Amendment to the United States Constitution guarantees an accused the right to assistance of counsel in his or her defense. This did not extend to the poor until the decision by the United States Supreme Court called *Gideon v. Wainwright* in 1964. That decision guarantees everyone charged with a crime—including those who are indigent and can't afford a lawyer—the right to be represented by legal counsel. My client, Darryl Thurston,[1] was charged with possession of four different kinds of controlled substances: cocaine, heroin, PCP, and marijuana. The marijuana was found in his coat pocket and was a relatively small amount. The other drugs were found in a shoebox in the bedroom closet. The thing was, it wasn't his apartment—it was his girlfriend's—so there was a real question about whether or not those drugs were his. I was assigned as his lawyer, but Darryl didn't want any representation. Just as a person has a right to be represented, he or she also has the right to represent him- or herself.[2] And that is what he wanted to do.

The judge, James Osgood, was not happy. A person representing him- or herself (called going *pro se*) was far more likely to mess things up, and the chances that a conviction would be reversed by a higher court were high. Judge Osgood tried all different ways to talk Darryl out of it.

"Do you know the old saying about representing yourself?" Judge Osgood practically harumphed.

"No, sir, I don't," Darryl replied in a respectful tone. He was in his mid-twenties, a medium-complexioned African American man with a soft, low voice.

"The lawyer who represents himself has a fool for a client!" the judge responded. "And you are not educated in the law. You really should reconsider."

Darryl smiled slightly. As the public defender assigned to Judge Osgood, I would be assigned to the case should Darryl change his mind. He was in custody, as he could not make the $50,000 bond that had been set in light of the charges (the heavier drugs all carried mandatory minimums of six years and a maximum of up to thirty years, of which a convict had to serve 85 percent if he didn't lose any good time). His criminal record didn't help either. It was long, albeit not violent—drugs, a burglary, and some disorderly conducts as well.

"Judge, Your Honor," replied Darryl, "you might be right. But I just don't trust nobody the state provides me. They the same folks trying to lock me up."

This was a problem with which I and my fellow public defenders were very familiar. It was hard to trust someone you thought might not really be a lawyer, someone paid by the county and whom you didn't pick yourself.

Judge Osgood shook his head in exasperation. "Okay, Mr. Thurston," he said. "You can represent yourself, but I am appointing Miss Lyon as standby counsel."

I almost exclaimed aloud, "No!" This was the worst of all worlds— I would be there to consult with Mr. Thurston, and thus clean up the record for the court, but was unable to actually do the case. It was like being in the back seat of a car being driven by someone who thinks he knows how to drive but does not.

Darryl and I met many times before his trial. I did the investigation he wanted done, including getting a copy of the lease to the apartment (which was in his girlfriend's name), showing and discussing police reports with him, sending out subpoenas for him. As I helped him, it did not appear to me that he was suspicious of me or that he didn't trust me. So finally, I asked him how he felt.

"Well, Miss Lyon," he said, looking down a bit, "I think you is a sincere person and would do a fine job."

I waited for the "but."

"But," he continued, "I can't take the stand 'cause of my record, and the jury can't get to know me if I don't." I nodded. "But if I try the case myself, maybe they will see I ain't a bad guy and cut me a break." He grinned. I could see his point. He was likeable, and maybe it would help.

He went to trial with me sitting in the audience pews and consulting with him during breaks. The jury acquitted him of all of the "heavy" charges, convicting him on the marijuana found in his coat. That carried a maximum of five years at 50 percent. Since Darryl had been in custody nearly eighteen months, that would mean another year.

I went back in lockup to congratulate him. I warned him that the judge would likely give him the maximum sentence. He told me he understood.

About thirty days later, it was time for him to be sentenced. After the judge heard from the prosecution and the probation department, he asked Darryl if he had anything to say.

"Yes, sir, I do," he replied. "You all should be thanking me right now." He nodded in a self-satisfied way.

"Thanking you?" said Judge Osgood sternly. "For what?" he added incredulously.

"Look around," said Darryl, "at everybody here." I looked around and noticed, hardly for the first time, that he was the only Black person in the room. Both prosecutors were white, I was white, the judge was white; so were the clerk, the sheriff, and even the police officers who had testified against him. "None of you all would have jobs if it weren't for me!"

I have thought about that many times. The War on Drugs was—and is—a big industry, what has been referred to as the prison-industrial complex. While it is common knowledge that white people use the same drugs at the same rate as Black people, this is never reflected in the courts. Black and brown people get arrested for having or selling drugs way more often than white people. In this book, I will discuss the truth of Darryl's pronouncement and how important it is that we as a country dig out from the mass incarceration business we have created— and never let ourselves go back.

One way to start to do that work is to create an office of a Defender General of the United States—an agency charged with the job of representing those who are affected by injudicious and racially biased policies but have no voice in the development of those policies.

There have been a handful of lawyers, legal scholars, and others who have proposed an office of the Defender General in the past, myself included. There are myriad ideas of what a Defender General should or could do. Some have offered defense needed at the United States Supreme Court level, to even the playing field between the interests of the government and the defendant.[3] Others have proposed that there be an official needed to push back on Department of Justice when their motivations for certain arguments in court are overly driven by the politics of the time; others, like me, have suggested that there needs to be a political counterbalance to the United States Attorney General.[4]

Darryl Thurston was right about a lot of things. Unsurprisingly, however, Judge Osgood gave him the maximum sentence allowed under the law.

1

You Have the Right to an Attorney—Kind Of

In that most ubiquitous of scenes on television and in movies, law enforcement read the familiar *Miranda* warnings to the bad guy, the person they have arrested.[1] You know the scene. Two cops come upon the criminal, catching him red handed, and he starts to place his hands behind his back almost before they ask him to. Then, in monotone, one of the cops rattles off the *Miranda* warnings, a routine he has done hundreds of times before. Usually, those rights are recited with an air of triumph, a way of saying, "We have you now." One of these rights is the right to an attorney, and that if the arrested cannot afford an attorney, one will be provided for free.

Those who work as criminal defense attorneys and prosecutors know the scene does not always unfold quite like this. In fact, whole cases are won or lost, or never even make it to trial, based on when and how *Miranda* warnings are delivered.

Nonetheless, this has become such a familiar trope in popular culture that some people may be surprised to learn that historically, a person who could not afford an attorney had *no* right to have one appointed. This was true until the landmark case of *Gideon v. Wainwright*, which established that right in 1964. Until then, the Sixth Amendment's enshrining of the right to counsel in our Constitution was believed to be one that could be exercised provided one had the means. This right, ensconced in the Bill of Rights itself, is more often breached than honored.

While these fundamental rights are promised by the Bill of Rights, what happens in real life unfortunately doesn't often look like those ideals. Because of this, many defendants are shortchanged and often

wrongfully convicted, wrongfully sentenced, or even wrongfully sentenced to death. This is what happened to Derrick Morgan.

Derrick was charged with a gang hit. The evidence against him
came primarily from a jailhouse snitch and an eyewitness. Neither witness's account was corroborated by any physical evidence, and in fact,
after the first trial, we discovered that the jailhouse snitch's testimony
couldn't physically have been the truth. The trial was a travesty from
start to finish. Derrick was represented by two Black attorneys, and the
judge was openly racist toward and about them and Derrick. He called
the lawyers "Laughing Boy" and "Smiling Boy" on the record. He also
once suggested that chambers needed to be fumigated after Derrick was
brought back there for a sidebar conference.

Because it was a death penalty trial, the jury was "death qualified,"
eliminating any juror who was against the death penalty. This meant
that anyone who expressed the opinion that they could not consider
sentencing someone to death was immediately pulled out of the jury
pool. The defense had requested the right to also "life qualify" the jury,
but the judge said no.

Life qualifying, as you may guess, would have excluded any jurors
who expressed the opinion that, if the defendant was found guilty, they
could not conceive of any sentence *other* than the death penalty. Well,
the judge said no to pretty much *anything* the defense asked for. One
juror was allowed to serve even though she stated during voir dire that
death was the *only* appropriate punishment, even though that is not
the law. At that time, there was no right to challenge such a juror for
cause—in other words, because they could not be fair in this case—but
Derrick's lawyers tried. Worse, the defense had no more peremptory
challenges (discretionary strikes allowed each side in a case) left, so
when the judge denied the defense's challenge for cause, she sat as part
of the jury.

During the trial, the judge shut down the defense at every turn. They
were stopped during cross-examinations, given time limits to make
their case, not given jury instructions to which they were entitled—it
was terrible. Derrick's rights were trampled on, and as a result, he was
sentenced to death. The direct appeal was denied, and Derrick's request
to life qualify the jury was given short shrift.

In fact, the Illinois Supreme Court chastised Derrick's appellate attorney for raising his appeal because it had been rejected so many other

times. Anyone sentenced to death had an appeal go to the Illinois Supreme Court automatically, rather than to an intermediate court. There, the Illinois Supreme Court affirmed. Alan Andrews represented him on appeal and filed a request to the United States Supreme Court to overturn the Illinois law that didn't allow life qualifying—and to everyone's surprise, the Supreme Court took the case, agreed with that position, and ordered a new sentencing hearing for Derrick.[2]

Because we assumed all appeals had been lost, I had started to work on Derrick's post-conviction. At the time, I ran the agency that represented death row inmates in post-conviction and federal habeas corpus matters, investigating cases and presenting any constitutional violations we found as a result. When the Supreme Court ruled on the life qualifying issue, I had to switch gears from a complete reinvestigation of the case to thinking about how to best represent Derrick at a new sentencing hearing. In my investigation, I learned of many details that should have been used at mitigation—which is the part of sentencing where the jury hears about reasons to punish with imprisonment rather than death. Mitigation can include any evidence that might tend to explain the client's actions, background, circumstances, family history, mental health issues, physical health matters, or the impact the client's execution would have on his or her loved ones. We also determined that some of the evidence introduced at the trial had to be false. All was not lost, however, in my investigative work, because we were easily able to use what I had learned so far in preparing for the new sentencing hearing.

One afternoon, I walked over to the jail to visit Derrick. It was the second or third time I had visited since the Supreme Court's reversal for a new sentencing hearing deciding whether or not he would be sentenced once again to death. I went through the normal bureaucratic rigmarole in order to see him.

In Chicago, there are many pretrial detention centers—eleven, actually: one houses women, one is the medical part of the jail, and the rest are for men. Derrick was in the "old" part of the jail, known as Division 1. At one time this was the only pretrial detention facility in Chicago. It is old, with peeling linoleum, mismatched bricks, and arcane naming conventions for parts of the facility. I went down to the basement to where Post 78 was—the most private place to see a client. It was, however, a bit haunting; it used to be the electrocution chamber. And then, there he was.

We had already met a number of times while I was working with Alan on the Supreme Court case brief, when I was about to begin work on the post-conviction petition, and once or twice after the remand to the trial court. But I had yet to have a substantive conversation alone with him.

Derrick sat in his jail beige uniform. We said our hellos, and I told him why I was there.

"I thought it might be time to start talking about this hearing coming up." I paused. "Are you clear on what the hearing is for?"

"I think so." He stopped for a moment. "It's death row—if I go back."

I nodded. That was a fair assessment of the situation.

"And what we are trying to do is to try to keep you from going back there," I said.

I went on to explain that in order to keep him from returning to death row, we needed to know everything about him—this would be for mitigation, where the jury evaluates everything about the defendant. The rules of evidence are relaxed at the penalty phase; in most states, this means that anything that is "relevant and reliable" is admissible. A capital defender thus faces the daunting task of investigating and preparing to meet the evidence against the client in the trial as well as investigating and preparing to meet the aggravating evidence—evidence of the client's prior criminal record, bad behavior while incarcerated, prior acts of violence, things about him that are bad and that might make a jury believe he is too far gone or too dangerous to live—at a penalty phase, in addition to locating and presenting mitigating evidence. Both mitigation and aggravating evidence are often a matter of shame to the client and his family. I explained this to Derrick the best I could, and then I handed him a series of release forms that would allow us to communicate with and receive copies of records from various entities—doctors, social service agencies, and the like.

Derrick looked alarmed as I handed him the papers. It became clear over the course of our conversation that he could not read them. I wish I could say that this is unusual, but unfortunately, the connection between people who are undereducated or have developmental deficiencies and those who get in trouble is well known and documented.[3] As it turns out, the why of Derrick's inability to read would play into the importance of mitigation in his case.

While I waited to learn more about Derrick for mitigation, I had other investigations for his case to get done: the prosecution's theory that made this into a death penalty case instead of noncapital murder was that it was a gang hit—a contract murder. There were plenty of inferences that would lead one to that conclusion, but the only direct evidence that this was a hit came from the ubiquitous jailhouse snitch. These guys are a fact of life in prisons and jails. If a guy who is looking at, say, ten years on a robbery can become an important witness on a more serious case—say, a potential death penalty case—he has something to bargain with. And that something was not the truth. I just had to prove that.

My investigator—the amazing Mort Smith[4]—and I were scheduled to go to the local jail in Michigan City, Indiana, to take a look around and to find out the names and types of the records they kept so we could subpoena them. It had been my experience that each correctional facility called records by certain idiosyncratic names. For example, one jail might call disciplinary records just that, while another might call them records for administrative review. If you didn't know the right name of the record, you would never get it.

Getting through security involved many people reading our permission letter many times, multiple phone calls during which we could hear suspicion in the guard's and staff member's voices, and what felt like inquisition-level questions regarding just what our purpose was in the building.

Finally, we were allowed in, and we followed a cheerful, beefy guard down a predictably linoleum hallway. I wondered if there is a color called "jail green"—it seems to be the corrections institution paint color everywhere. Not quite pea soup, and not quite lime; it is somewhere in between, almost as if someone made a sauce using pea soup and lime. On the walls, it looks just about as appealing as it sounds. The hall twisted and turned, and then we followed the guard up a flight of stairs to the tier. "The elevator's down," he said. "Second time this week."

We walked on to the tier and stopped dead in our tracks. Yes, Derrick had been in cell one and the snitch in cell two; this we knew. But what we did not know—and what we could not have known without going to the jail—was that tier had a floor-to-ceiling steel wall, easily two feet thick, that stood between the odd-numbered cells and the even-numbered cells. The snitch had testified that he and Derrick talked between the cells. But to have that conversation between these two particular cells, Derrick would have needed to shout and the snitch would have needed to shout back—both through the two-foot-thick steel wall! Of course, proving that the so-called statement from Derrick could not have been made didn't guarantee a finding that the homicide was not a contract killing. A new sentencing jury might still find that the killing was a hit based on the circumstantial evidence. But this new evidence—that it was physically impossible for Derrick to have made that statement—would certainly help our case.

I was encouraged, and I was reminded why we must always visit the tier, retrace the steps, walk the stairways, traverse down the alleys, and look through the windows—the tiers, steps, stairways, and alleys where people claim things happened a certain way. We must take these steps to either validate or refute that they could have happened that way. It also helps in trial preparation, because if you know how it felt, looked, and smelled, you are going to be able to paint a better picture for the jury. And there is one other message: If I went to the scene, it means I care about the client. I was also even more motivated now to find out how Derrick had come to travel on his own path, the path that had once led him to death row.

A few weeks later, I received a call from Derrick's sister. He had told her to call me—a good sign that he trusted me and wanted me to know things about him. I spoke with her by phone and eventually, with some encouragement and prodding, she agreed to meet me at a McDonald's close to her neighborhood. I arrived early, and to my surprise, so did she.

We talked for a long time. She told me that she and Derrick and their siblings (three girls, two boys, all "bunched up together") had lived with their mother in various apartments on the South Side of Chicago. After I listened for a while, some things became clear: At about nine years of age, Derrick's older sister, Darlene (now deceased), was the caregiver, and Derrick, starting at around age eight, stole to feed himself and his siblings.

Before he was even twelve, Derrick was recruited into a street gang. *Recruited* is perhaps the wrong word; he was coerced. What we know now—and what is supported by multiple scientific studies—is that coercion and undue influence impact adolescents differently than they do adults, based on brain development and maturation.[5] How else was he to eat? To provide for his siblings?

This was hard to listen to. Here was this little family of children taking care of themselves. "Derrick, he was doin' stuff in they turf, you see." She paused. "He didn't have no choice. He had to pay up, which we didn't have no money, or join up. So he did." She shook her head ruefully. Things got better, she explained, once he joined—because he could steal more easily and get protection, but that meant he would sometimes be gone too. And he began to do really poorly in school—to the degree that any of them went—and to have headaches. That reminded me. I had noticed when Derrick turned his head to the right, it seemed that there was a square indentation on his forehead. When I asked Darlene about that, she said she knew he got hit by a bread truck, but I would have to get more information about it from Derrick.

I followed up on what I had learned. It turned out that Derrick had indeed been hit in the head by a bread truck, and the square marks I saw on his forehead were where the truck's mirror from had hit him—hard enough that he lay bleeding on the street and was still unconscious when EMTs brought him to the hospital. He was stitched up, but no neurological work was ever done on him. Most telling was that in the second grade, at age seven, his IQ tested at 90—low normal. At age nine, in the third grade, it was only 70, right at the level where he would be classified as having mental retardation. And the accident? It happened when he was eight years old.

Derrick confirmed what his sister had told me about their life, but every time he did so he was careful to tell me that he didn't blame his mother—that she had her troubles too. When I finally told him about the IQ tests and what our expert would say about them, I must say I was nervous. It can't be easy to hear "You are mentally retarded," and it was worse still to know that this information would become public at the new penalty phase sentencing hearing. So after I told him, I just sat quietly, letting him think about it. He was looking down, shaking his head. I braced myself—would he swear? Yell? Deny it? Accept it?

He looked up. "I didn't know," he said softly. "I thought it was my fault. I couldn't do it—couldn't read, couldn't remember shit—it was like—it was like . . ." He stopped, choked up. "It ain't my fault, is it?"

"No."

"You gonna tell this?"

"In court, you mean?" I asked.

"Yeah."

"Yes. It will help win the sentencing hearing."

In 2002, the United States Supreme Court held that it was unconstitutional to execute someone with mental retardation.[6] However, when I was working with Derrick, it was considered perfectly fine—and in fact, the state of Illinois has executed at least one mentally retarded man. But this evidence still helped explain Derrick's poor decision making and might engender some sympathy or understanding. And coupled with his terrible upbringing, it should count.

This isn't to say that Derrick was not responsible for his actions; he was. But the choices he made are not the same as the choices made by those of us fortunate enough to have a supportive and stable upbringing and without intellectual deficits to contend with, and that should have made a difference.

And it did make a difference. Derrick was not sentenced to death. At the time of the imposition of the prison sentence by the judge, Derrick was asked if he wished to say anything. He did.

"Your honor, I just want you to write down on that paper, to please give me some help—I never knowed I was"—he couldn't say *retarded*—"you know . . . an' I—you think that you could write it down to get me help? So I could do better?"

The judge swallowed hard a couple of times. He looked at me and nodded. "Sure," he said. He swallowed again. It was so sad.

What happened to Derrick Morgan in his original trial representation is that he got neither the fair, impartial trial he was due under the Constitution nor the level of representation to which he was entitled. Why had his original lawyers not found out about the wall between him and the jailhouse snitch? Had the state known that information—and hidden it? These were violations to Derrick's right to due process and adequate representation—and they are are all too common. With overwhelming caseloads and limited resources for public defense and no consequences to the prosecution or police when they hide information that would aid in acquittal, the system does not result in anything like justice. If there were standards and consequences—something a Defender General could work to establish—maybe Derrick Morgan wouldn't have spent years on death row, contemplating his death. A Defender General could help train capital defenders so that those attorneys would know that they had to look for evidence of physical or psychological damage—or, as in this case, both.

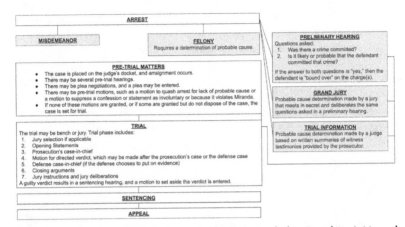

Figure 1.1.   Arrest to Appeal. *Lyon, et. al.*, Post-Conviction Practice: A Manual for Illinois Attorneys, *Illinois State Bar Association (2012). Graphics redesigned by Samantha Farmer, college student at Purdue University.*

Figure 1.2.   Proceedings. *Lyon, et. al.*, Post-Conviction Practice: A Manual for Illinois Attorneys, *Illinois State Bar Association (2012). Graphics redesigned by Samantha Farmer, college student at Purdue University.*

As discussed at the beginning of this chapter, the right to an attorney wasn't a part of the US legal system until 1963. So where did this extension of the right to counsel to the poor come from? Here is the story.[7]

The Sixth Amendment provides:

In all criminal prosecutions, the accused shall enjoy the right to a speedy and public trial, by an impartial jury of the state and district wherein the crime shall have been committed, which district shall have been previously ascertained by law, and to be informed of the nature and cause of the accusation; to be confronted with the witnesses against him; to have compulsory process for obtaining witnesses in his favor, and to have the Assistance of Counsel for his defence.[8]

For a long time, the right even to *present* a defense wasn't assured under the law in England, the country from which the United States imported a lot of our common law.[9] Criminal offenses were viewed as private matters handled between the purported victim and the person accused. There was not even a prosecutor, let alone a defense attorney![10] This changed in the 1730s, when representation by counsel became more common, but there was still no guarantee a defendant could have an attorney.[11]

Here, prosecutors developed their role within the system early on, but defendants still had no guaranteed right to an attorney until after the American Revolution—and those who could not afford an attorney went without.[12] During the drafting of the Sixth Amendment to the US Constitution (it was ratified in 1791),[13] the Framers moved away from the idea that a judge could adequately represent a defendant who did not have counsel.[14] Not only did the Framers have a strong mistrust of the paternalism that was considered a norm in English common law, they were also skeptical that the government could or would act in the best interest of the defendant. Imagine that! In all seriousness, the Framers appeared to understand that a defendant's interests were best served by providing him with tools to act on his own rather than just assigning someone to take over.[15] Can you imagine the same person who is deciding a defendant's case also providing him or her with a defense? That is indeed how it was until the authors of our Constitution decided that a "defendant's interests were best served by providing him with the tools to determine and act in his own self-interest."[16]

After this, things sat for quietly for a while. There were relatively few Supreme Court cases that addressed Sixth Amendment issues until the early to mid-twentieth century.[17]

As Sixth Amendment jurisprudence started to take shape, the Supreme Court recognized in *Powell v. Alabama* that "it is hardly necessary to say that, the right to counsel being conceded, a defendant should be afforded a fair opportunity to secure counsel of his own choice."[18] Lower courts have taken the opportunity to reverse based on failure to provide choice, but this choice is often very limited. For example, a defendant may *not* insist on being represented by an attorney who has a potential conflict with the opposing party. In *Wheat v. United States*, the Supreme Court held that although "the right to select and be represented by one's preferred attorney is comprehended by the Sixth Amendment," that right can be outweighed by the judicial system's "independent interest in ensuring that criminal trials are conducted within the ethical standards of the profession and that legal proceedings appear fair to all who observe them."[19] In 1938, the United States Supreme Court held in *Johnson v. Zerbst* that indigent criminal defendants in *federal* court were entitled to counsel.[20]

In 1942, the Supreme Court first spoke to not only the right to have a lawyer (again, only in federal court) but the right to have a lawyer who could do the job and who did the job. In *Glasser v. United States*, that notion began to take hold, starting with the idea that one shouldn't be represented by a lawyer who had conflicting interests.[21] But these decisions didn't apply to the vast majority of criminal cases at all, since the states were responsible for prosecuting most cases. In fact, the Bill of Rights wasn't even considered to apply to the states until much later, in the 1960s with the advent of the Warren Court and beyond, when Sixth Amendment jurisprudence really began to take shape.[22]

Enter *Gideon* in 1963, guaranteeing the right of legal counsel to anyone accused of a crime.[23] Both criminal defense attorneys and those charged with a crime celebrate *Gideon v. Wainwright* for its mandate that indigent clients be afforded counsel.[24] While counsel was originally intended only to assist defendants in their own defense (as the accused saw it), these roles shifted over time.[25] At a minimum, counsel must give their client the authority to decide whether to plead guilty or not guilty, whether to have a trial with a jury, and whether or not the defendant will testify. Each of these three key decisions is rooted in a clear constitutional right and cannot be taken from the defendant by a lawyer's decision alone.

A number of cases throughout the 1960s and later began to strip away at the autonomy of defendants by giving wide decision-making discretion to counsel and making it exceedingly difficult to challenge those decisions to a higher court.[26] The greatest example of granting a great deal of deference to the lawyer came twenty years after *Gideon*, in *Strickland v. Washington*,[27] where the Court defined what *effectiveness* means: not very much. Some lawyers joke (with a certain amount of bitterness) that it is the legal equivalent of the "foggy mirror" test:

If the person representing the defendant was a lawyer and if you held a mirror up to his or her nose it would fog up, that was enough. When analyzing whether a defendant received that constitutionally guaranteed counsel, courts do not want to play Monday morning quarterback, even on bad strategy, so they are deferential to the job done by an attorney and do not disturb convictions on that basis very often.

In order for a convicted person to succeed with an ineffective assistance of counsel claim, a defendant must prove (1) that counsel's performance fell below an objective standard of reasonableness and (2) the substandard representation so prejudiced the defendant that there is a reasonable probability that the outcome would have been different.[28] A defendant does not have to show that the outcome more likely than not would have been different, but rather that counsel's errors undermine confidence in the outcome.[29]

The effect of this standard is that it has become a floor below which lawyers may not fall rather than a standard to which they should aspire. When attorneys do just enough to get by, it most times results in terrible outcomes for clients, wrongful convictions, and injustice at every turn. Yet the law does not require more. Worse yet, even if a court finds that a lawyer's performance fell below that floor, to succeed in getting a new trial the defendant must show prejudice: that the defendant was hurt by the ineffective representation, and that the result at the trial might have been different otherwise.

There are many examples of how poorly a lawyer may perform and still not fall below the standard of reasonableness. For example, the United States Supreme Court refused to hear a case where the Court of Criminal Appeals of Texas held that counsel's sleeping through parts of his client's death penalty trial could have been a strategic move. Seriously—sleeping through trial could be considered strategy? The Court also held that the presence of counsel at all times during trial, combined with a failure to show prejudice, did not mean the defendant was ineffectively represented even though he was convicted and sentenced to death.[30] In other words, he was worthy of death; so what if his counsel sloughed off a bit here and there? In another example, the Illinois Supreme Court held that presenting conflicting theories to a jury—such as, "He didn't do it. But if he did do it, he cannot be held responsible because he is insane"—was *not* ineffective assistance of counsel. The court affirmed the conviction and death sentence in that case.[31] Any reasonable person would think these behaviors fell below a standard of ordinary care, but the courts did not.

Because courts grant such wide deference to attorneys, most claims of ineffective assistance of counsel fail. Courts defer to "strategic choices" by defense counsel—even foolish ones. Usually, the only claims that have any chance of being successful are failure to investigate claims. But for those claims to succeed, someone must discover that there has been a failure to investigate in state post-conviction proceedings.

Defense counsel's overarching duty is to advocate the defendant's case.[32] Counsel also has a duty to bring to bear such skills and knowledge as will render the trial a reliable adversarial testing process.[33] In other words, "[A]n attorney who fails to even interview a . . . witness [who] may potentially aid the defense, should not be allowed automatically to defend his omission simply by raising the shield of 'trial strategy and tactics.'"[34] Unfortunately, this happens all of the time. Defense attorneys defending their own bad behavior place nearly everything they do within a case in the "trial strategy" bucket—and most times, they get away with it.

Although on paper, the rights afforded by the Sixth Amendment are absolute and must be afforded to the client, the wide deference discussed above has created a whittled-down set of protections for defendants. Further, this deference makes it very difficult to prove that counsel was ineffective. So a person may be guaranteed a lawyer, but they are not guaranteed a *good* one, nor are they guaranteed the right to be in charge of their own case or be able to make a successful claim if their lawyer fails them.

So that is the background of how the United States moved from granting a person charged with a crime no rights to some rights—sort of. Unfortunately, the promise of *Gideon* has yet to be fulfilled. In fact, it is likely that the proponents of this right of representation did not foresee that not only the poor but also minority defendants must be represented, which means that at least some of the social and racial concerns of the accused—concerns that had been previously ignored—became a part of the consciousness of the courts, albeit only with great reluctance.

The fact that public defenders and appointed lawyers are most often representing communities of color as well as poor whites means that the concerns of the defense and those communities are belittled and marginalized—or at least they have been historically. This is not solely the fault of those public defenders, who are almost unilaterally under-funded, taxed with unimaginable caseloads, and looked down upon by others within the system. Everyone, poor or not, has the right to a law-yer. Not only that, defendants have the right under the US Constitution to effective assistance of counsel. That right is limited, though.

For defendants who are poor or without means, the choices are ex-tremely limited. Those who cannot afford counsel are subject to the locally run systems for providing public defense, giving the defendant little choice in the matter. For example, in *Morris v. Slappy*, when a defendant requested one public defender over another, the Supreme Court rejected the claim that "the Sixth Amendment guarantees a mean-ingful relationship between an accused and his counsel."[35] Instead, the Court held that so long as a defendant's rights were upheld, it was less important who was assisting the defendant.[36] The Court later explained in *United States v. Cronic* that "the appropriate inquiry focuses on the adversarial process, not on the accused's relationship with his lawyer as such."[37] So people who cannot afford to have choice get what they get, and any later claim must be based on ineffective assistance rather than on the fundamental constitutional protection that may have been breached.

So what does the right to a lawyer really mean? Does it mean merely the presence of defense counsel, or something more? In other words, is this a right in form only, and not "real"? Defendants who are in a posi-tion to hire counsel and pay to have a team working for them receive a certain level of treatment. Those who cannot afford that get much, much less. But, the system argues—and the courts affirm—that what they are getting is "better than nothing."

Another problem is that while a defendant who cannot afford a lawyer is assured one, this right stops after the direct appeal of a con-viction. Consequently, most post-conviction petitions are filed pro se, usually by inmates of correctional institutions who cannot perform an investigation even if they had the skills and resources to do one. In other words, indigent inmates who are poorly represented in the first place cannot likely succeed in state post-conviction. And since the advent of the Antiterrorism and Effective Death Penalty Act of 1996 (AEDPA),[38] they cannot raise issues for the first time in federal court, either. If the prosecution can make a credible case that defense counsel could have presented or preserved a fact or claim at the trial level but did not, that fact or claim is waived.[39] If appellate defense could have raised a fact or claim on direct appeal and did not, it is waived.[40] If a fact or claim could have been raised in state post-conviction or habeas and was not, it is waived.[41] While none of this was new when AEDPA passed, since the rules on waiver had been getting tougher as death penalty jurisprudence had progressed in the 1990s, the act greatly increased the burden on defense counsel. Until AEDPA, there was sometimes a way around the problem of waiver.[42] Imprisoned inmates or those sentenced to death who could show that they had both cause for the failure to present the fact and the federal claim to which it was tied and could show prejudice to them as a result, could overcome the procedural roadblock and at least get to present their issue to the federal court.[43] After AEDPA, this was no longer the case. Now inmates must show not only cause, but innocence as well.[44]

Perhaps you've heard of all those "technicalities" that get the "guilty guys off." Well, it's actually these technical rules that make it nearly impossible to get them out, even if they are innocent. For example, in one case in Virginia, defense lawyers filed their request for relief using the mailbox rule, which holds that as long as your documents are postmarked in time, they are on time—kind of like when you file tax returns. Up until that time, this had been standard practice in Virginia, but the courts ruled in Roger Coleman's case that although the appeal was mailed within the required thirty days, because it was not received until three days after the deadline, he had forfeited the right to be reviewed.[45] The federal courts found that procedural bar—filing three days late— prevented them from reviewing the case.[46] Coleman was executed.

Imagine that you go to see a doctor and the doctor comes in and tells you, with great sorrow, that you have a rare disease; there is no treatment and no cure. She tells you to get your affairs in order, as you have only three to six months to live. Devastated, you leave the office and start trying to do just that. Then, about a month later, you see in the news that there is a new medicine that can cure you. With great joy you go back to the doctor and say, "Doctor, I am cured! I can get this new medicine!" What if she told you that you could not because when you were diagnosed, there was no such medicine? That is what I mean by the limitation that convicted individuals face in their uphill battle toward justice. If there is a new law or new facts that haven't been presented to the state courts that are found after the filing deadline, then you *never can* present that information—no matter if you are innocent.

So what is the answer? Because "effectiveness" has been so diluted by the courts, and is, in my view, so inconsistent with our constitutional obligations to our clients, we as defense lawyers must hold ourselves to a higher standard of effectiveness at the trial level. Effective representation requires a team; it requires investigation, motions litigation, and creative thinking, and not an assembly-line mindset.[47]

I realize that providing good representation requires more of our ever-scarcer resources,[48] but might it not also mean that we would have fewer wrongful convictions and fewer costs, both financial and societal, that those engender?

In a study of the costs of wrongful convictions, John Conroy and Rob Warden documented that

[w]rongful convictions of men and women for violent crimes in Illinois have cost taxpayers $214 million and have imprisoned innocent people for 926 years, according to a seven-month investigation by the Better Government Association and the Center on Wrongful Convictions. . . . The joint investigation, which tracked exonerations from 1989 through 2010, also determined that while 85 people were wrongfully incarcerated, the actual perpetrators were on a collective crime spree that included 14 murders, 11 sexual assaults, 10 kidnappings and at least 62 other felonies. Moreover, the 97 felonies in that crime spree may be just a fraction of the total number of crimes committed by the actual perpetrators. The investigation found that the 85 exonerations left 35 murders, 11 rapes, and two murder-rapes with no identified perpetrators and thus no way to add up their accumulated crimes.[49]

Although there are many causes for these wrongful convictions—including prosecutorial, police, and forensic misconduct,[50] as the report found—bad, ineffective lawyering had a role as well.

In my view, ineffective lawyering compounds each of the causes of wrongful convictions listed above. Why do I say that? Because it is investigation, thorough motions practice, and zealous advocacy that is the greatest check on our system. If someone is pushing hard for *Brady* material (evidence that would cast doubt on the defendant's guilt—which is unfortunately often excluded, whether intentionally or not, by the prosecutor during discovery), insisting on litigating the admissibility of evidence or the right to present a defense, and asking

Causes of Wrongful Convictions

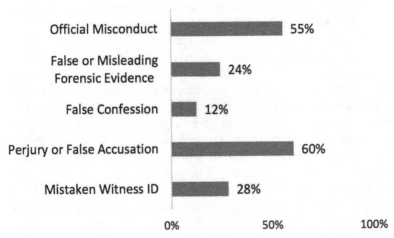

Figure 1.3.   Wrongful Convictions. *Graph created by E. Kate Cohn. Data from National Registry of Exonerations, retrieved 9/6/2021. https://www.law.umich .edu/special/exoneration/Pages/ExonerationsContribFactorsByCrime.aspx.*

the tough questions both in and out of court, there is a smaller chance of the other causes of wrongful conviction prevailing. Most of these strategies utilize extensive motions practice—asking the court to rule in a certain way. Motions can run the gamut from something as simple as a request for discovery to something as critical as a motion to forbid the prosecution from asking for the death penalty. Cases are often won or lost based on the extensive and thorough approach a lawyer takes to motions, and this work takes time.

This kind of advocacy is impossible to do when caseloads are monstrously high, resources like investigators and experts are in short supply (or nonexistent), and the view prevails that where there is smoke there is fire, and if the defendant didn't commit *this* crime, he or she probably did something else. Effective assistance of counsel is in the best interest of all of us, not just the accused. A society that cannot trust its criminal justice system fails.

Having a law license and showing up to court to say something—be it stupid, unsupported factually, or misguided legally—and doing the bare minimum (perhaps between naps) is not the quality defense anyone would want for themselves or someone they love. In many, if not most, systems that provide representation to the poor, that representation is negatively impacted by low salaries, high caseloads, and lack of respect from the courts, the opposition, the public and, unfortunately often the client community. If minimal due process would not be good enough for you, it should not be good enough for anyone else. It is time for us as a nation to pick ourselves up from the floor.

This is difficult to do, however, as our constituency is hardly a popular one. No one roots for people charged with crimes, just as no one truly presumes innocence. It is counterintuitive to do so. If there have been a number of break-ins in your neighborhood and you read that the police have arrested someone, you don't think to yourself, "Ahh! I presume him innocent!" It is far more likely—and understandable— that you would say to yourself, "I'm glad they caught the guy!" After all, where there is smoke there is fire, right? Add to this the specter of racial stereotypes, conscious and subconscious, and the presumption of innocence recedes even further.

The presumption of innocence, receded by stereotypes and road-blocked by the lack of resources provided for defendants, is even further exacerbated by the public and the jury's perception of how crime and criminals are portrayed in entertainment and the news: mugshots, movies, TV shows, one-dimensional defendants.

If you ask most people where they get their information about the criminal justice system, they won't say newspapers, civics class, or even news magazines—they will say the local news and television programs, in particular the ubiquitous and long-running *Law and Order* television program and its spinoffs.[51]

These programs have predictable qualities to them: there is a victim, a bad guy (the "perp"), and the forces of good who arrest or exact revenge on the one-dimensional bad guy.[52] The victim is also one dimensional:[53] pure as the driven snow or too young to have discernable faults.[54] And the news follows suit.[55]

While no one deserves to be attacked violently, those who have been attacked are not always without some fault or participation in what happened to them. For example, if a person is robbed at gunpoint, that is awful and a crime and should be punished. But it is relevant to our understanding of that crime if the victim was flashing money around in a poor neighborhood while buying drugs. It doesn't mean he deserved to be robbed—no one does. But where he is and what he is doing is not irrelevant. In an instance such as this, did the victim's actions contribute to the robber's choice of victim? Absolutely.

It is no more irrelevant than the fact that the robber may be the eight-year-old breadwinner for a family of seven children—of which he is the second oldest and his sister, the primary caretaker of the children, is only nine years old—when there is no adult on the premises; the various fathers are uninvolved with the children, and their mother is an addict. I represented this young man later in his life after he was (forcibly) recruited into a gang, and you met him earlier in this chapter: Derrick Morgan. Did he commit a crime? You bet. Did he deserve to die in prison or as a result of execution? No, he did not.

Then you also have the juror's perception, which is with them from the moment they are seated and see the defendant sitting at the table. When jurors come into a courtroom, they do so with certain scripts in their head.[56] Their life experiences, upbringing, and education all help them to function in the world, and that means that they expect certain events to happen a certain way.[57] If the elevator light shows "up," they expect that the elevator is going up.

Similarly, they walk into a courtroom with expectations about crime, courts, and criminals—but their life experiences, upbringing, and education are not necessarily where they get those expectations. In all likelihood they have little or no contact with the criminal justice system personally, have not studied it in school, and weren't brought up around folks with personal or educational knowledge about it.[58] So where do those expectations come from? The news and television crime drama, that's where.[59]

Even assuming a given juror has no particular political viewpoint about crime, has no hidden agendas, and is otherwise a blank slate, social science tells us that he will believe that "dark is dangerous,"[60] that the police always get the right guy, and that the prosecutors are knights in shining armor.[61] Even if this hypothetical juror intellectually knows better, the only *stories* he has heard on the subject are from these sources, not from his own experience or that of anyone close to him.

So this potential juror will not know that a young Black man from a tough neighborhood learns early not to wait around to find out what the police want—to run whether they have done anything wrong or not.[62] It will not have been his experience that a rite of passage to adulthood is to

have his father or mother explain to him how to behave *when*—not *if*—
he is stopped by the police: to not make any sudden moves and to use
the words *sir* or *ma'am* in order to avoid getting shot.[63] He won't know
of anyone doing someone else's time or how easy it is to be mistaken
for someone you are not.[64] In other words, his life history will not help
him to look critically at the news or crime drama, and he will likely be
unaware of its effect upon him.[65]

An individual accused of a crime follows a path or road. There are
multiple curves and turn-offs in the road, depending on the crime, the
circumstances, and the person him- or herself. But certain parts of the
path are traveled by everyone—or at least they should be: *Miranda*
rights and the right to counsel; a good, thorough trial preparation based
on thorough motions practice and a quality investigation; the ability
to strike jurors who demonstrate bias; the introduction of mitigating
factors that provide context to a defendant's own life experience; then,
a remedy available when convicted, based on the right to appeal and
make claims of ineffectiveness, and renewed investigation for post-
conviction. These are the markers along the path. Each of these steps
should be protected, and someone like Derrick should be afforded rights
and guidance and good counsel at each step of the way.

In the vast majority of cases, however, this does not happen. Instead,
at every turn, defendants are provided the minimum, if any, of the rights
that should be afforded to them. Public defenders have immeasurable
caseloads, leading to minutes—mere *minutes*—spent preparing to defend those accused of heinous crimes. Defense counsel also calls the
shots, often at the expense of providing any autonomy to the defendant:
"Trust me." "I know best." "I am working for you." "Nonstop attention,
that is what you are getting." Attorneys, both private and public defenders, make these statements all the time—meanwhile, they sleep through
trial or bill for hours they actually spent at the bar down the street.

This is where a Defender General comes in. Looking at things from
a structural level, the Defender General is missing from the United
States government. And no, the Defender General will never defend
the likes of Derrick Morgan—but the Defender General will look at the
roadblocks that cause Derrick and others like him to be so ill served by
the system.

Just like a person accused of a crime travels the road from *Miranda*
to the highest level of appeal, so too must the Defender General, as-

sessing and then addressing the issues highlighted here and in the chapters to come. An Office of the Defender General can present a strong case for many parts of this path—like perhaps setting standards so that Roger Coleman would not have been executed for following the "mailbox rule."

Yes, change takes time. And yes, more roadblocks will appear before some go away. But we need someone trying to address these issues, and right now, there are only small pockets of dedicated individuals, working tirelessly, but in disparate groups, bubbles, and silos, often at the local level. The Defender General can learn from these groups, and the work can happen up and down the chain.

This is why there needs to be an Office of the Defender General of the United States—a place where these issues can be advocated for, where legislative travesties like RICO and AEDPA (discussed in chapter 5) can perhaps be stopped in their tracks by an institutional office that represents the poor and the disenfranchised, where there are standards for representation that are supported by training and appropriate grant-making; in other words, an office that sees to it that when someone is arrested and told he or she has the right to an attorney, it actually means something.

2

The System Isn't Broken; It Was Built This Way

To those who do not work within the criminal justice system and are not in any way touched by the system—particularly socioeconomically privileged white people in the United States—it may appear that the system works just fine. A crime is committed, it is investigated, and someone is arrested and has his or her day in court. A judge or a jury evaluates the evidence and applies the law, and, if appropriate, the individual is convicted and sentenced. Justice is served fairly and swiftly.

In fact, what happens is far more haphazard. Although some cases are well investigated, most are not. It starts with *Miranda* rights at the time of arrest. As described in chapter 1, those rights are guaranteed by the Fifth Amendment to the US Constitution and were affirmed as case law doctrine in *Miranda v. Arizona*.[1] The confession—whether obtained properly or improperly—forms the basis of many, if not most, prosecutions.

As the public is starting to see, false confessions occur far more often than one might think. *When They See Us*, Ava DuVernay's 2019 limited series on Netflix, brought renewed attention to one of the most well-known false confession cases: the Central Park jogger case.[2] In 1989, a female jogger was found brutally attacked and raped in Central Park. The crime caused an uproar in New York City, and police were under pressure to find those responsible. Five Black and Latino youths, aged fourteen to sixteen—Kevin Richardson, Antron McCray, Yusef Salaam, Raymond Santana, and Korey Wise—who had been seen in the park that night were arrested for the crime and interrogated. Under intense police questioning, four of the boys admitted to roles in the crime and implicated others. But the youths also gave conflicting accounts of the crime, and none of the DNA evidence matched any of them. All of them later said they were coerced into giving false statements. After years in prison, all five men were exonerated when a serial rapist confessed to the crime and his DNA tied him to the crime scene.[3] While the great amount of attention given to this case is appropriate—as the case was, and is, an anomaly—most cases with false confessions go undiscovered and are certainly underreported.

In fact, most Americans believe that there is no such thing as a false confession because they have an innate belief that no matter how much force, coercion, or trickery was used against them, they wouldn't confess to something they didn't do.[4] But false confessions are much more common than one might expect. The National Registry of Exonerations had tracked twenty-four hundred false confession exonerations as of March 2020. Nearly 40 percent of exonerations based on false confessions were for defendants who were under eighteen years old at the time of arrest, and 70 percent had a reported mental illness or intellectual disability.[5] What the police did to the Central Park Five happens all the time, especially when police feel they can "get away with it."

Coerced confessions are just one way in which police engage in misconduct. Indeed, a major cause of wrongful convictions is prosecutorial and police misconduct, including confessions and other bad acts. The New Orleans prosecutor's office is infamous for this. John Thompson was awaiting execution when investigators found that prosecutors had withheld exculpating results of a blood test. In other words, the police had evidence showing he was innocent but didn't turn it over, even though it is required by law. He ultimately was freed and sued for prosecutorial misconduct, where he won at the trial level, but the United States Supreme Court reversed based on the doctrine of prosecutorial immunity, which protected the prosecutors.[6]

John Floyd spent thirty-six years in prison for the murder of a newspaper proofreader before it came to light that someone else's fingerprints and DNA had been found at the scene. Reginald Adams spent thirty-four years in prison for the murder of a police officer's wife, only to be freed after a police report implicating a different man was found buried in unrelated case files.[7] You might think that the prosecutor's office that did this—deliberately—would be held accountable. Unfortunately, you would be wrong.

In fact, in *Connick v. Thompson*, the Supreme Court held that "plaintiffs who seek to impose liability on local governments under § 1983 must prove that 'action pursuant to official municipal policy' caused their injury."[8] As might be expected, Justice Ruth Bader Ginsburg dissented in the case: "A district attorney's deliberate indifference might be shown in several ways. . . . [District Attorney] Connick created a tinderbox in Orleans Parish in which *Brady* violations were nigh inevitable. And when they did occur, Connick insisted there was no need to change anything, and opposed efforts to hold prosecutors accountable on the ground that doing so would make his job more difficult."[9] When those on the inside see no need to change, why would they? Instead, they perpetuate a culture that allows for, and maybe even encourages, misconduct at every step.

And this culture does not start in the district attorneys' offices. The gaps and omissions in education and training prior to lawyers entering the field also helps fuel what Justice Ginsburg referred to as the inevitable "tinderbox."[10]

The current landscape of ethics education in law schools is critiqued as being underdeveloped.[11] A study published in the early 1990s stated that fewer than 2 percent of the pages of law school casebooks consisted of ethics-based content or discussion.[12] Further, some critics offer that the teaching of ethics has been cordoned off to one professional responsibility course,[13] often taught in such a formal manner that true ethical quandaries are not introduced for discussion.[14]

A troubling illustration of unsanctioned complaints can be seen in the Washington State data, as one example. The results of the most recent American Bar Association (ABA) Survey on Lawyer Discipline Systems, from 2017,[15] demonstrate that fewer than 5 percent of complaints filed with the ABA in Washington State resulted in sanctions for attorneys.[16] In Washington State, the decision-making boards are mostly constituted by attorneys.[17] In 2017, only 29 percent of the board members were nonattorneys,[18] leaving little outside attention and guidance toward this accountability mechanism. As discussed above, attorneys are not likely to report the unethical or illegal behavior of their own colleagues, and therefore, the majority-attorney composition of these state boards is problematic. So with little training in law school and no true accountability mechanisms within the ABA, of course the tinderbox will flame.

This glaring example of culturally accepted and culturally encouraged misconduct is one more example of where a Defender General could step in: working with prosecutors and providing education, training, and accountability mechanisms regarding conduct.

Given the natural human reaction to presume guilt—especially when the accused is an "other"—improper conduct makes giving an adequate defense even harder. And even when a defendant has a lawyer, it is no guarantee of a good and fair defense. There are many mind-boggling examples—such as the lawyer sleeping though part of his client's death penalty trial, discussed in chapter 1—of poor lawyering that was found *not* to be bad enough to require a new trial (i.e., ineffective assistance of counsel).[19]

But counties and cities also fail in more subtle ways at their obligation to provide effective counsel to the poor. For instance, some municipalities contract with the lowest bidder from a private firm to do this representation; as a result, some clients are assigned to offices where the firm gets paid less than $6 an hour after covering overhead.[20] This would hardly motivate anyone to adequately investigate, prepare, and try a case, or to even do a creditable job at a sentencing hearing.

And the defense, particularly for the poor, can be equally or even more haphazard. When I was a public defender assigned to a felony court in the 1980s, I was responsible for more than 220 felonies myself at one time. Unfortunately, the issues of work burden and caseload have not changed. In many states the numbers are even worse, and the poor are effectively denied access to justice. How can one human being investigate, write, and file pretrial motions, and do a good job for her clients under circumstances like that? The answer is that one cannot, not for every client, and frankly, not for most. The Tommy Braxton case is illustrative of these issues.

The Henry Horner Homes were a housing project on the Near West side of Chicago. Built in the late 1950s, they were eventually demolished in 2010. These projects were known as some of the most neglected in the city—and some of the most gang-ridden.[21] They housed many gang members from many gangs, some affiliated and some not, and violence and drug dealing were common. The Chicago Police Department had a small satellite office in an unused first-floor apartment, and officers assigned there knew the projects well. They knew Tommy

Figure 2.1.   The Henry Horner Homes are no longer standing. *Photo by Patricia Evans, https://www.chicagoreporter.com/dismantling-the-towers/.*

Braxton (not his real name) very well. Whenever there was trouble, odds were high that Tommy did, saw, encouraged, or knew all about it. He was the quintessential "usual suspect," and police would pick him up as a matter of course whenever anything happened there.

By the time Tommy had a case before Judge Maroni (also an alias), his record reflected several fights, drug charges, and arrests that didn't end in conviction. Like so many poor and nonwhite defendants, Tommy's case landed with me, the public defender assigned to Judge Maroni's call. In an underfunded and overworked office, I did as much as I could for my clients; but over the course of my career, I represented thousands of clients—disproportionately poor and disproportionately nonwhite—who were all but adjudicated guilty the day they were arrested. Tommy's case was not atypical.

It wasn't a "big" case; it was a burglary of a house a mile or so west of the projects. After being assigned, I went into the lockup to meet my client for the first time. Judge Maroni sat in one of the large courtrooms at 26th and California, now the Leighton Criminal Court Building, where most criminal cases go.

Figure 2.2. **26th Street. The grand courthouse is surrounded by jails.** *Photo taken by Andrea D. Lyon.*

The building is west and south of downtown, surrounded by eleven county jails that house thousands of people like Tommy, who are held in jail pretrial only because they cannot make bail. As the Bail Project notes:

> On any given day, nearly half a million people languish in jail cells across America, waiting for their criminal cases to move forward and severed from their lives and communities even though they have not been convicted of a crime. People in pretrial detention now make up more than two-thirds of America's jail population. They are presumed innocent under the law, yet they will suffer the harms of incarceration unless they have enough money to pay bail and buy their freedom. This two-tier system criminalizes poverty and is a structural linchpin of mass incarceration and racial inequality. It affects entire communities, devastates families for generations, and guts the presumption of innocence.[22]

The lockup, the where inmates are held while visiting the courthouse for their hearings, was always crowded. I preferred to see my clients in the jail, where we could have a private meeting. However, this wasn't what Tommy wanted, even as I explained to him why I didn't think it prudent to discuss his case in front of so many people.

"Miss Lyon, is it?" he asked. (Did I mention his voice was one that carried?)

"Yes, Mr. Braxton," I replied.

"Look here," he said. "I'm just Tommy and they got me hooked up here 'cause I wouldn't give them no information. I ain't done this burglary or whatever and they know it." I started to respond, but Tommy rushed on. "Look, them police always come get me for whatever go down in Horner." He shook his head ruefully. "Tell the truth, they right most of the time." He grinned at me infectiously. "I get in a lot of trouble. You know, fights and what not."

He cleared his throat. "But I ain't done this, and they arrested me 'cause they wanted info on a murder of this guy in Horner, he a big time GD [Gangster Disciple] who go by Beastie." I assumed that was his street name and nodded to Tommy to continue. "I *told* them I ain't know nothing about it, but they didn't believe me. Especially not Carrot-top."

I would learn later that this was the Horner nickname for an Officer Gillespie (not his real name), whose hair was more orange than red. "So, they told me they gonna give me a case. And that is just what they done did."

"Tommy," I responded, "I want to know more about all this, so let me come over to the jail to talk to you in two days. By then I should have at least some of the police reports and we can start talking strategy and investigation."

I hoped I wasn't lying to him. As one of two public defenders assigned to Judge Maroni's courtroom, I was responsible for more than two hundred felonies at any given time, as was my partner. The caseload was crushing, and investigating all my cases wasn't possible. Small cases usually settled, and a burglary fell into that category. Still, I wanted to try to do right by all my clients, and I figured the least I could do was go see him, find out what I could, and hopefully find a way to work on his case.

One evening later that week, at around 6 p.m., I went to Division 6 of the Cook County Jail and into an attorney room. Tommy came in. He was grinning ear to ear. "I ain't expect you would actually come," he said. I understood why he thought that.

So we discussed his case, and I got subpoenas served for the burglary and the homicide. It turned out that there was precisely nothing tying Tommy to the burglary other than the fact he could get to the victim's house by bus. The witness who called the police gave a description of a young Black man, about 5-foot-8, with medium complexion and build. While that description fit Tommy, it also fit at least a third of the other men living at Henry Horner. There were no other witnesses, no confession, no fingerprints, or physical evidence—nothing. I figured there must be a police informant or something, but Tommy insisted that the charge was given to him because he wouldn't say anything about Beastie's death.

The reports from that case showed that Beastie was shot in a gangway between two of the Horner buildings, where his body was found, shortly before 11 p.m. on the night of the burglary. He had been shot in the chest and the stomach and bled out. Although lots of people heard the shots, no one saw anything. That isn't atypical in shootings where gangs are involved; being a witness could be dangerous.

Interestingly, the Beastie reports listed Tommy as having been interviewed. He was labeled uncooperative by Officer Gillespie and there was a handwritten note on the side of the report that Tommy was to be "transferred to property crimes per discussion." That was unusual, to say the least, and it bolstered Tommy's claims. This information was gathered slowly over several months. I didn't get to see my client again other than in the lockup on court dates; I just didn't have time. I was trying cases, pleading out most of them, and trying to keep up.

Tommy's case was unusual insofar as I was nearly certain of his innocence. In cases where defendants are guilty (as in cases where defendants are innocent), police misconduct is far more common than you'd think. In 2018, body camera footage appeared to show a Staten Island police officer briefly turn off his camera in order to plant a lit marijuana cigarette in a Black teenager's car.[23] The officer claimed that his camera experienced a technical glitch and he was never charged. With or without video evidence against them, police officers are awarded nearly universal benefit of the doubt, assumed to be righteous agents of the state inherently above immoral agendas. With the power of prosecutors on the side of the police, much misconduct never sees the light of day.

I was also worried that the general description that Tommy fit would result in an in-court identification. For the vast majority of juries, the mere presence of an in-court identification is enough to look past shoddy evidence.

There are a lot of well-documented reasons for the frequency with which misidentification leads to wrongful conviction, both because of the inherent difficulty in identifying a stranger and sometimes as the result of unintended or deliberate police misconduct during identification procedures. Decades of scientific research and real-life cases have shown that eyewitnesses can make mistakes.[24] In fact, data from DNA exonerations demonstrate that mistaken identifications are a leading cause of wrongful convictions.[25] The National Registry of Exonerations has identified 532 individuals exonerated by DNA evidence proving that they did not commit the crimes for which they were convicted,[26] and the Innocence Project reports that individuals exonerated by DNA evidence spent a combined total of more than four thousand years in prison. Critically, mistaken eyewitness testimony played a role in approximately 69 percent of these cases.[27] Thirty-two percent of the cases involved multiple eyewitnesses who wrongly identified the same innocent person as the perpetrator.

Certain police procedures can also increase the chance of mistaken identifications. Given the implications of these mistaken identifications, eyewitness memory researchers have examined factors that may reduce the possibility of mistaken identification. Specifically, researchers in the field of eyewitness memory have cautioned that certain lineup procedures may be more likely to produce mistaken identifications; as such, they have recommended against using these procedures.[28]

Scientific studies have demonstrated that jurors find eyewitness testimony to be a convincing form of evidence.[29] Further, more than thirty-five years of research finds that members of the legal community—jurors, defense attorneys, prosecutors, law enforcement officers, and judges—generally misunderstand a number of the factors that can influence an eyewitness's identification.[30] Put simply, some legal professionals hold beliefs about eyewitness memory that are in direct opposition to the scientific research.

Even when suggestive identification procedures are acknowledged by a trial court, a witness could still be allowed to identify the defendant in court if the initial, contaminated identification is deemed reliable based on five factors: "the opportunity of the witness to view the criminal at the time of the crime, the witness's degree of attention, the accuracy of his prior description of the criminal, the level of certainty demonstrated at the confrontation, and the time between the crime and the confrontation."[31] The problem with relying on these factors—referred to as the *Manson* factors after a 1977 United States Supreme Court decision—to adjudicate reliability is twofold. First, research has demonstrated that some of the factors can be manipulated by faulty police practices, and that the list excludes many relevant indicators of reliability.[32] Second, and more crucially, the *Manson* factors reduce reliability to a checklist—a fundamentally flawed way to make a determination on an issue as sensitive and case specific as witness reliability.[33] Reliability should be not assumed if one can "check a box"; witness identification is much more nuanced than that. Indeed, legal scholars, attorneys, eyewitness experts, and law enforcement alike can appreciate the complexity of eyewitness identification and can agree that misidentification is easily achieved, even with the best of intentions.[34]

On Tommy's fourth court appearance, I filed a special motion for discovery for information about any related cases, and moved for any documents that would show relation between violent crimes and property crimes. I also filed a motion to dismiss the charges due to police retaliation, which was such a long shot it seems hardly worth mentioning. Pretrial discovery requirements vary from state to state, but most states require that the prosecution turn over to the defense certain standard materials. These generally include a list of witnesses and their addresses; any statements made by those witnesses, the defendant, or any codefendants that are not work product; any expert reports; and any material or information tending to negate the guilt or punishment of the defendant. The defense also has a right to examine all physical evidence, and the prosecution has a continuing duty to provide discovery as it becomes available.

A general discovery motion is usually filed in any criminal case, and I had done that at the beginning of Tommy's case. But my request for more—with the clear implication that there was police misconduct—did not please Judge Maroni. He made sure I knew that he had hundreds of cases on his call (true), that many were very serious (also true), and that he wasn't going to waste his time on a penny ante damned burglary. I tried to explain that "just a burglary" was important to my client, who could go to prison for seven years if convicted. Judge Maroni was practically sputtering by then. So I requested a hearing. Everyone in the courtroom seemed to be a combination of amused and annoyed. The case was continued for a hearing in a month, but the air quotes for the word "hearing" were visible to me, even though no one actually used them. (It wasn't unlike when you asked your parents to go somewhere, and they answered "maybe" but you knew that meant "no.")

When I went back to the lockup behind the courtroom, Tommy was angry. He didn't appreciate the dismissive way the judge and the prosecutors responded to my requests, and flat-out asked me if he had any chance in front of this obviously biased judge.

"I have to tell you, Tommy," I replied reluctantly, "I don't think so. What we are alleging—that you are being wrongfully prosecuted—is unusual, and the law isn't great. Prosecutors are given a great deal of leeway on whom they charge and with what, and courts really don't want to interfere with their decision making."

I didn't know how to explain that there was a decades-long trend of deference to prosecutorial discretion working against him. Prosecutorial discretion is the power of a prosecutor to decide whether to charge a person for a crime and which criminal charges to file. Today, it is a broad power that also gives prosecutors the authority to enter into plea bargains with a defendant, which can result in the defendant pleading guilty to a lesser charge or receiving a lesser sentence for pleading guilty to the original charge.

Prosecutors may have a variety of reasons for exercising prosecutorial discretion. They can choose not to file charges, to drop charges, or to offer a plea deal when the circumstances surrounding the crime warrant it. Probably one of the biggest advantages of deferring to prosecutorial discretion is that it promotes judicial economy by making things run more smoothly. It also allows them to secure cooperation from defendants who "turn state's evidence," which is in the interest of the prosecution. But what it also does, more often than not, is encourage pleas from defendants for things they did not do or for which there would not actually be a winning defense. When the cards are stacked, defendants will often cut their losses rather than take a gamble. And the gamble is essentially—and sometimes actually—with their life.

There are almost no limits on the powers of prosecutors, which blurs the line between discretion and abuse. Probably the biggest downside of prosecutorial discretion is that it creates the potential for selective prosecution. Because of the inherent subjectivity of prosecutors' decision making, their personal beliefs and biases—whether conscious or unconscious—can creep into their decisions.[35] Knowing that Tommy's prosecution was based on bad faith wasn't the same as proving it. To do that, I needed more evidence, which is why I filed the motion for discovery.

"So, what you even file the motion for, then?" he asked, his tone both challenging and defeated.

"Because it is the right thing to do, even if it's tilting at windmills."
Tommy looked puzzled. I didn't consider that my literary reference
probably sounded as inaccessible as the foreign language of legalese
he had been forced to endure in the hearing. I shook my head and explained the *Don Quixote* reference before I continued: "And I believe
you. You are usually a good bet for the police—that you are involved or
know what happened, right?" He nodded. "I think they were just pissed
at you because they were going to have to actually work to solve this
case." I paused reflexively, deciding if I was going to tell him God's
honest truth. "And there is another reason. Look, there isn't enough
time to do things around here. I have too many cases. The prosecutors
have too many cases and so does the judge. If they think I might gum
up the works with motions practice, they may consider dismissing or
pleading the case way down just to get rid of us."

Sure enough, the prosecutors asked me what Tommy would take.
A part of me wanted desperately to take the case to trial—to make the
prosecution try to prove Tommy's guilt beyond a reasonable doubt with
one witness's vague recollection, to make them call Officer Gillespie
to the stand and expose, on the record, his obviously corrupt note that
Tommy be "transferred to property crimes."

But my responsibility was to get the most favorable outcome for
Tommy, not to unmask police misconduct. I had to be frank with
Tommy about what going to trial would actually mean. He couldn't
possibly find the $5,000 cash to post bail, so that meant at least six more
months locked up. He wouldn't be able to earn money, see friends or
family, or enjoy his basic freedoms. On top of this, trial outcomes are
considerably worse for folks who are unable to make bail.[36]

And there was another thing. If Tommy's case made it to trial and
he was convicted, his sentence could likely be far harsher than if he
pleaded guilty to the same charge now. Those of us in the legal field call
it the trial tax. System-wide, judges are likely to hand down more strin-
gent sentences as punishment for wasting the judicial and prosecutorial
resources associated with a trial. Risking a higher sentence is simply
too costly for many defendants, especially for defendants of color and
lower socioeconomic status. While punishment for exercising one's
Sixth Amendment right is unconstitutional, it's also the norm.

The emergence of the trial tax can be detected in the steady decline
of trial rates (and corresponding uptick in guilty pleas) throughout

the twentieth century. Originating as hush-hush agreements between prosecutors and defense attorneys in the later part of the nineteenth century,[37] plea bargaining quickly replaced trials as the dominant legal arbiter. Albert Alschuler recorded federal guilty plea rates of 77 percent in 1936, 80 percent in 1938, and 86 percent in 1940.[38] By 1990, 14 percent of federal convictions were decided by trial and by 2000, that number was just 5 percent.[39] The same trend holds true in state courts. The National Center for State Courts found that 2015 felony trial rates in California, New York, and Texas were 2.3 percent, 4.0 percent, and 2.1 percent, respectively.[40] Today, the rate of criminal convictions that were decided by trial is around 3 percent nationally, leaving 97 percent decided by guilty plea.

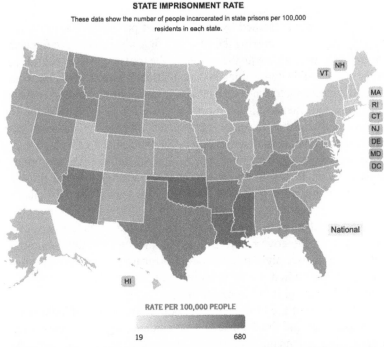

STATE IMPRISONMENT RATE

These data show the number of people incarcerated in state prisons per 100,000 residents in each state.

RATE PER 100,000 PEOPLE

19   680

Figure 2.3.   State Imprisonment Rate. Darker shading indicates a higher rate of incarceration. *https://www.sentencingproject.org/the-facts/#map?dataset-option =SIR. This interactive website allows users to see incarceration rates by state and also view racial disparities and juvenile sentencing statistics.*

The guilty plea determines conviction rates, and there are, in turn, multiple states that have high rates of per capita incarceration.[41]

Long gone are the days of clandestine plea negotiations. Pleading guilty and pleading early is now expected, normalized, and procedurally reinforced in courtrooms, thanks in large part to the trial tax making the alternative too risky. In *Missouri v. Frye*, the Supreme Court quoted scholarship articulating unequivocally that plea bargaining "is not some adjunct to the criminal justice system; it *is* the criminal justice system."[42]

In these 97 percent of criminal convictions, defendants yield rights that are hallmarks of the US criminal justice system. Along with a guilty plea, defendants are often required to forgo their right to challenge unlawfully procured evidence and their right to an appeal.[43] Most importantly, when defendants waive their Sixth Amendment right to a trial, the state is absolved of the responsibility to prove them guilty beyond a reasonable doubt.

Instead of being saddled by the burden of proof, the government is running the show by making the cost/benefit analysis lean toward pleading guilty. Prosecutors with the weight of the trial tax on their side all but unilaterally decide convictions in "negotiations" with the defense. Even though judges tend to sentence well below guideline maximums, judicial discretion to sentence higher can be a powerful point of leverage for prosecutors.[44] Further, the ease of getting a conviction can disincentivize prosecutors' obligation to presenting a fair and diligent case.[45]

As prosecutors secure more power against defendants, the protections inherent to a trial disappear. Defense attorneys spend most of their time negotiating plea deals instead of advocating for their clients' rights.[46] The pressure to plead quickly can prevent sufficient investigation into exculpatory evidence. Without a trial, judges cannot scrutinize the legality of the government's case.[47] Without a jury, the public cannot execute its oversight role.[48] And unfortunately, the criminal justice system in the United States is more committed to judicial efficiency than it is to justice. It minimizes trials, not errors.[49]

In the vision of the Framers—and codified into constitutional law—the prosecution and the defense present evidence and arguments before a court. The defendant is presumed innocent until proven guilty, and the prosecution is required to prove guilt. Today, the trial tax disincentivizes the defendant from exercising that right. It literally undoes the protection offered by the Constitution in the name of efficiency.

I asked Tommy if I should negotiate his case down. I thought it was possible I could get him a time-served sentence on a misdemeanor like criminal damage to property. His record was pretty extensive, so one more misdemeanor wouldn't affect him all that much. He agreed, the energy leaving his body like the air out of a just-popped balloon, and Tommy's misdemeanor became one of the 97 percent of criminal convictions that never go to trial.

I knew I had, in criminal justice parlance, done well by him. But it felt terrible. The police had punished him for not doing what they wanted and were going to get away with it. No one but us would ever know.

In the first chapter, I discussed the path individuals take when accused of a crime. Along the path, there are the way things "should" work and the way things "should work." Yes, I am repeating the phrase, purposefully. Some people—defendants, legal scholars, attorneys, and activists—feel the criminal justice system *should* reflect the promises made by the US Constitution: the right to an attorney, the right to remain silent, the right to a trial, the right to plead guilty or not guilty, the right to confront witnesses. But others—judges, prosecutors, and the police—see the broken system working exactly as it should. They want "bad guys" put away. They want judicial efficiency. They want to tout that from arrest to sentencing, they are tough on crime. The result? The system is working just as it should—in some people's eyes.

Sometimes I hear people say, "This is not how the system is supposed to work." But actually, it is designed to work exactly this way. The ideal of the prosecution being required to meet a burden of proof and letting the public see what the police, prosecution, and courts are actually doing remains just that: an ideal. This means not only having a voice at the policy table and addressing the disparity in the defense and prosecution functions in terms of resources, but being willing to change our culture. We need to imbue the defense function with the same gravitas and essential nature that we do law enforcement, prosecutors, and judges. This can be done, but only if there is a method for ensuring it is done. A Defender General of the United States would provide those of us who stand by the side of those accused the same respect as the Department of Justice and the judiciary.

We need major policy changes that will ensure sufficient resources to both prosecute and defend cases. This means having all voices at the table, not just those of law enforcement and political expediency. We need a Defender General of the United States.

3

[Un]equal Justice

Racism's Thumb on the Scales

Many, if not most, of us have had the experience of saying something without thinking about it first and realizing its truth (and sometimes its importance) as we say it. My experience with that came at a career day at a junior high school in Chicago.

You remember career days, right? Adults, often parents of other students, join assembly or homeroom or take over a PE class for the day. One is a nurse, another is a dentist, and another, a truck driver. They share the details of their job, how they landed in that career, and what schooling they have had, and try to show some excitement as they drone on about how you too could be in the career they have chosen. Truth be told, to a junior high student, these presentations are not inspiring—in fact, they are usually downright dull. I certainly remember rolling my eyes during some of these presentations.

But now here I was, on the other side of things, at an all-Black junior high school, in line to speak to sixth and seventh graders about being a lawyer. My talk was a little more interesting, though; at the time I was a public defender in Homicide Task Force, which is a unit that represents persons accused of homicide, and defending murder cases was certainly more interesting than cleaning teeth. At that time, women were still quite unusual in our profession, so that was interesting too.

I told the students about the charging process and how those of us in the homicide division got our new cases: We showed up on our assigned day in Branch 66, where all of the preliminary hearings on homicides and sex cases were held each day; when it was our turn in line, if the person charged with homicide didn't have and could not afford a lawyer, that person became our client. We learned all about the case and the client, prepared motions, investigated and prepared for trial, and tried the case. I told the students a little about what it was like to try a case where so much was on the line. Then I thought it was time for questions.

I asked if anyone has any questions, and one seventh grade girl asked me a very thoughtful—and, as it turned out, profound—question. "When you get a new case" she asked, "what is the first thing you want to know?"

Without thinking, I said, "What color is the victim."

I looked at my audience and saw them all nodding. These *children* already knew that their lives were considered less important than others, and that race determines what happens to you and for you. It is well known that if the deceased is white, punishment is more severe, convictions are more likely,[1] and a fair trial is less likely. It broke my heart.

I wish I could say that this has changed, but in truth it has not, as anyone following the news in recent times knows. The murders of George Floyd, Breonna Taylor, and far too many others to name; the wrongful convictions of so many people of color; the inability of people in the system to see gray—all of these matters tell us that racism negatively impacts our criminal justice system. While this is hardly news to most of us who defend the accused, the question is why and how—and more important, what can we do about it now?

Much has been written about the history of policing coming out of slave catchers and the discrimination that was a part of the law in criminal statutes in the infamous Black codes.[2] Racist policing has its roots in Black codes, which has its roots in slave codes.[3] Slave codes were created to even further restrict the actions and behaviors of slaves, in part to control them and prevent uprisings.[4] Virginia was the first of the colonies to enacts slave codes, and most others followed suit.[5] But once slavery was abolished, weren't the slaves codes also? Well, yes—and no.

Black codes swiftly replaced slave codes as the Thirteenth Amendment established supposed freedom for all.[6] When President Andrew Johnson implemented Reconstruction policies starting in May 1865, all states had to uphold the abolition of slavery. There was also a requirement to pay off war debts and swear loyalty to the union,[7] but not much else.

As a result, state governments had a lot of freedom in rebuilding their own governments, and from these, Black codes were born. Black codes were used to control Black Americans, allowing southern whites nearly the same level of social control they enjoyed during slavery.[8] Whites controlled employment practices, wages, and other economic freedoms. For example, in Mississippi, Black people had to show evidence of employment for an upcoming year each January, and if they left a job before their contract was up, they would forfeit wages and were subject to arrest.[9] Once a law was broken, it was as if the Black person was enslaved again, and forced labor was allowed as punishment for a crime.[10]

Eventually, Congress passed the Civil Rights Act of 1866.[11] But even though the act granted all citizens the "full and equal benefit of all laws and proceedings for the security of person and property,"[12] the Black codes continued. And this leads us to today, when the stops, frisks, monitoring, surveillance, and arrests of Black and brown people are used as a form of social control.

How the progression from slave codes to Black codes to racist policing and prosecution plays out in the system is less well known, certainly to the majority of Americans whom it doesn't directly affect. For example, the general public now has much sympathy for addicts because of the opioid crisis and its slide into heroin and fentanyl addiction, and that is because the vast majority of those addicts are white. During the 1980s, however, during the crack crisis, where the addicts were mostly Black and brown, addiction was more often considered a moral failing rather than a disease. We see this play out everywhere. A person carrying bread during Hurricane Katrina's aftermath is either a looter (read: Black) or "finding" supplies for his family (read: white).

In the criminal justice system, this plays out in many ways. There are more frequent stops, searches, and arrests in Black and brown communities, but that does not equate to higher drug use in those communities.[13] Instead, these individuals start to build a lifelong criminal record for actions that go unnoticed and unstopped in white communities. Further, these records involve harsher sentences, because prosecutors are twice as likely to pursue mandatory minimums for Blacks, as compared to whites charged with the same offense.[14] And as we know, Blacks are often stereotyped as violent addicts and are more likely to be killed by law enforcement, who are reacting to stigma and racism more than the individual situation they are responding to.[15]

Then there is the "perp walk": the handcuffed defendant paraded in front of the media. Prosecutors and law enforcement use the perp walk

Figure 3.1. Hurricane Katrina. This image was accompanied by the caption, "A young man walks through chest-deep flood water after looting a grocery store in New Orleans, Aug. 30, 2005." *AP Photo/Dave Martin.*

Figure 3.2. Katrina. This photo was captioned, "Two residents wade through chest deep water after finding bread and soda from a local grocery store after Hurricane Katrina came through the area on August 29, 2005, in New Orleans, Louisiana." *Getty Images/Chris Graythen.*

for various ends, such as to show the public that law enforcement is doing its job or that the defendant is being treated in a suitably humiliating fashion.[16] Even though some legal scholars have argued that the perp walk should be considered a statement and therefore not in alignment with professional standards required of prosecutors (specifically, for "making extrajudicial comments that have a substantial likelihood of heightening public condemnation of the accused"),[17] the perp walk continues.

In a decision rejecting a § 1983 civil rights challenge to a perp walk, one court said that the practice serves the legitimate function of educating the public as to the seriousness of law enforcement, thereby serving to deter others from committing crimes.[18] Yet we know that not all accused individuals exposed to the humiliating perp walk are found guilty. Not all arrestees subject to perp walks have been convicted, and the accused individuals are entitled to a presumption of innocence under our criminal justice system.[19] Far from upholding the fairness and integrity of the system, the perp walk actually further conflates the charging stage with the verdict stage, undermining the importance of a hearing before a fair and neutral tribunal, which is supposedly central to our notion of justice. It is as if the verdict has been returned before the jury can even hear the case.

As we know, racist policies and practices obliterate each part of the accused individual's path. These practices certainly do not end after biased policing, arrests, and perp walks. It is interesting, however, to explore another trajectory within the criminal justice system that can be traced back to Reconstruction. When dissecting prosecutorial immunity, for example, we find a current cadre of case law, policy, and practice rooted in post–Civil War law that has turned out to be exactly the opposite of what it was supposed to be.[20] Let me explain.

Prosecutors are almost always granted absolute immunity from civil damages in lawsuits based upon their conduct undertaken in pursuance of their prosecutorial functions.[21] This creates an environment where the prosecutor can essentially do no harm. In fact, the United States Supreme Court solidified this provision in *Imbler v. Pachtman* in 1976: "The common-law immunity of a prosecutor is based upon the same considerations that underlie the common-law immunities of judges and grand jurors acting within the scope of their duties."[22]

But how did this protection start? What if I told you that it started in an effort to protect newly freed slaves? In 1871, Congress enacted United States Code 42 U.S.C. § 1983, also known as the Ku Klux Klan Act.[23] (Note that § 1983 is also discussed above regarding a challenge to the perp walk. A § 1983 claim is a civil action for a deprivation of rights.[24] So when an individual is wronged in the course of their criminal process, § 1983 is the best shot they have at making a civil claim—but it is an uphill battle.)

The Ku Klux Klan Act was passed with the intent to prevent unjust prosecution of federal officials who were assisting newly freed slaves with civil rights claims.[25] These officials were often victims of malicious prosecution in states that opposed Reconstruction efforts.[26] At its inception, drafters of § 1983 intended to use the federal statute to hold prosecutors civilly liable for malicious prosecution. In essence, Congress enacted § 1983 during Reconstruction to help enforce compliance with the Fourteenth Amendment and protect officials from frivolous tort actions at the hands of anti-Reconstruction prosecutors.[27] Okay, so far this makes sense. There were federal officials trying to help newly freed slaves. And there were malicious prosecutors out to get those federal officials, using bad charges to trip them up and prevent their efforts. So the Ku Klux Klan Act was intended to protect these officials from the malicious prosecutions. Okay. With me so far? But how did it end up protecting those prosecutors?

While § 1983 protected various categories of federal officials, and in practice was supposed to help protect those implementing Reconstruction, prosecutors were eventually protected as a class about twenty-five years after the statute was first adopted.[28] In 1896, the Supreme Court of Indiana held in *Griffith v. Slinkard* that, despite known malice committed by the prosecution, the civil action should be dismissed based on absolute prosecutorial immunity.[29] *Griffith* granted total exemption to the prosecutor, disregarding the alleged motivation behind the conduct.[30] In *Griffith*, the prosecutor maliciously indicted a defendant even though the grand jury had found no evidence or probable cause.[31] The court found the prosecutor's actions to be undertaken as a judicial officer, although not as a judge of a court.[32] Further, the *Griffith* court quoted a prominent treatise from the time:

> Whenever duties of a judicial nature are imposed upon a public officer, the due execution of which depends upon his own judgment, he is exempt

from all responsibility by action for the motives which influence him and the manner in which said duties are performed. If corrupt, he may be impeached or indicted; but he cannot be prosecuted by an individual to obtain redress for the wrong which may have been done. No public officer is responsible in a civil suit for a judicial determination, however erroneous it may be, and however malicious the motive which produced it.[33]

Over time, *Griffith* grew to become the majority rule on the issue,[34] even though it was a state case. And nearly a century later, the United States Supreme Court solidified immunity for prosecutors in *Imbler*.[35] Paul Imbler spent years in the California courts appealing a death sentence for a murder he did not commit.[36] After ten years of litigation, Imbler was a free man, which set the stage for his civil suit against the prosecutor in his case, among other governmental officials.[37] Even though Imbler's conviction was vacated on the basis of egregious state misconduct,[38] his resulting civil suit did not provide him with relief.[39] Instead, the United States Supreme Court summarized its position on absolute immunity by quoting Judge Learned Hand:

> As is so often the case, the answer must be found in a balance between the evils inevitable in either alternative. In this instance it has been thought in the end better to leave unredressed the wrongs done by dishonest officers than to subject those who try to do their duty to the constant dread of retaliation.[40]

The Supreme Court's analysis was based on the premise that common law immunity was "well settled."[41] The Court went on to ask the question of "whether the same considerations of public policy that underlie the common-law rule likewise countenance absolute immunity under § 1983."[42] They held that it did.[43] The progression demonstrates how a common law misnomer was invoked and clung to by the judiciary as a whole in order to make absolute immunity for prosecutors a majority rule.[44]

So there you have it. The trajectory of the federal statute demonstrates that its original intent was flipped on its head, as § 1983 was first adopted in 1871 to protect officials who were helping to ensure that individual civil rights were protected during Reconstruction.[45] However, a handful of state courts began to interpret this statute as a method to provide absolute immunity to prosecutors,[46] and this slow shift in the use of the statute leads us to the present day. A statute first enacted to protect individuals' civil rights is now being used to provide prosecutors with absolute immunity from civil liability.[47] Scholar and immunity expert Margaret Johns summarized the disingenuous way in which § 1983 evolved:

> [A]nd it certainly did not intend to insulate prosecutors from liability for malicious prosecutions, since that was one of the tactics of southern defiance to Reconstruction that the Ku Klux Klan Act was intended to remedy. To the extent that the doctrine of absolute prosecutorial immunity purportedly rests on historical understandings, it is insupportable.[48]

So now we have racist policing and prosecutorial immunity, which protects racist practices, and both have their roots in slavery and the post–Civil War period. Shocking? Maybe not. Maybe it just further drives home the point that when activists say the system is working as it is supposed to, we should believe them. The system is simply repackaging and redelivering the race and class hierarchies upon which this nation was founded.

I saw these race issues play out in my work as well. When I worked at the public defender's office in Chicago, I found that stereotypes and prejudice are problems for everyone, not just the prosecution or the judiciary—although it was more acute there.[49] I entered the office thinking that public defenders were liberal (which is, in my mind, a good thing) and thus "good" on race issues. Not so much.

There is no person without prejudices, myself included. Let me illustrate what I mean with an anecdote. I was in my tenth year or so at the office and a supervisor in the Homicide Task Force, which is a unit that represents persons accused of homicide. When I was a line member of the unit, I carried between twenty and twenty-nine murder cases at any given time, about one-quarter to one-third of which were death penalty cases.[50] The task force was a vertical representation unit, meaning that we picked up the case and client in preliminary hearing court and traveled with them wherever they went. Most of the office, however, provided horizontal representation—the assistant public defenders were each assigned to represent all indigent folks who came into a particular courtroom—despite efforts to implement vertical representation in all cases.[51]

With such a large county and office, horizontal representation provided the easiest form of organization. But one of the problems for client relations is that by the time clients work their way up to the felony courtroom, they have been in several courtrooms and have been represented by a number of different lawyers in the office. A single defendant has probably appeared in bond court, made one or more appearances in preliminary hearing court (where he may have been represented by a different public defender each time), and also appeared in arraignment court. If he is detained, it is unlikely that he has been visited by a lawyer at the jail (and most indigent clients cannot make bond), so the defendant often appears in the felony courtroom between three to six weeks later with only in-court representation.

Although I was a supervisor, I did not supervise the lawyer I am about to discuss. I will call him Paul. He was a white man in his late forties or early fifties—a career public defender. He was back in the lockup talking to a client, as was I. Behind every courtroom in the criminal courts are lockups where pretrial detainees wait until their cases are called. This particular lockup is about fifty by twenty feet, with open bars that allow defenders to approach their clients and speak to them through the bars with no obstruction. There is a "privacy panel" with a toilet toward the back. It isn't very private, and you learn to ignore it and not "see" it.

On this day, I was trying to speak to my client again about the motions we were filing and report to him about an investigation. Since these lockups are not very private—there can be as many as thirty or forty men (usually all men of color) back there—I told my client that

Figure 3.3.   The Lockup. *Photo taken by Andrea D. Lyon.*

we would discuss everything more fully when I came to see him at the jail later that week. But I could hardly even say that much, because Paul was yelling at his client nearby. From what I could gather, this client had been arrested sometime later than his codefendant. Paul had worked out what he believed was an advantageous plea for the codefendant. I am sure it was a good plea deal, but he was meeting this client for the first time and was trying to strong-arm him into taking the deal, which was apparently a package available either to both codefendants or to neither. Paul called his client stupid. He used pejorative terms such as "mope" and "ignorant gangbanger." He told the client that he—the client—could "do six [years] standing on his head"—and worse.

I was pretty sure Paul would never have spoken to a white eighteen- or nineteen-year-old in the same demeaning way. The two men were yelling at each other, and the entire lockup was listening.

I was not Paul's supervisor, but I asked him to step out of the lockup with me. I wanted to tell him that he was being disrespectful and that even if this was the best deal for the client, the client had no confidence in Paul and he was making it impossible for the client to maintain any sort of pride and accept it by fronting him off like that. I did not want to do the same to Paul, though, which is why I asked him to step out with me. He turned to me and snapped that he was busy. I told him I was too, then proceeded to say everything I had intended, adding, "Paul, this man is the reason you have a job. Show him some damn respect." Paul was furious with me, and I made a permanent enemy that day.

Later that week, I recounted this incident at a supervisors' meeting and suggested that we do something about the office and what I perceived to be conscious or unconscious racist attitudes coupled with the burnout that this work engenders. I said, "We all have prejudices—me too—but as public defenders, we should try to at least know that and account for it in some way." I asked my colleagues if they thought Paul would have perceived this young man as being able to do six years "standing on his head" if he had been white, middle-class, and from a suburb. My comments were dismissed as being overly sensitive (read: female) and the meeting proceeded to other matters. I looked around the room and realized that there were only one or two women or people of color in our ranks. Maybe that was the problem.

After the meeting, one of the African American supervisors told me that I "had done it now." I asked him what he meant. "It's one thing if

I speak about race," he replied. "It's viewed as self-interest. But if you do it, it is viewed as betrayal."

When I went out to my car that night, both front tires had been slashed. I will never know for sure if it was related to what I said in that meeting, but I have my suspicions.

In another example, I was a part of a team that ultimately freed a client from prison. This client, who was just barely sixteen when he was arrested, was tried as an adult under the automatic transfer laws in Illinois at the time, which placed children as young as fifteen, sixteen, and seventeen into adult court for charges like armed robbery, rape, and murder, with no consideration of their youth. Our client was African American. While automatic transfer for certain crimes is no longer required for fifteen-year-olds,[52] at the time, the location of a child's trial was one of the charging decisions made by the prosecution. Had our client—who was homeless and the victim of child sexual abuse—been charged with second-degree murder rather than first-degree murder, he would have most likely been kept in the juvenile system, where he could get treatment and help.

But no one besides us, his defenders, saw him as a child. The prosecution described the victim as having been in a "relationship" with the defendant, when the older man was in fact raping the defendant while providing him with food and shelter. At his trial, the defendant's lawyer had not presented use of force to defend against the forcible felony of rape. It is likely his own lawyer didn't see him as a child either.[53]

These are just a few of the ways race comes into the process. Another part of the trial where race and racial prejudice (both explicit and implicit) play an outsized role is in jury selection. The term *jury selection* is a bit of a misnomer; selecting a jury is actually a process of elimination in which a group of potential jurors (in some places, from voter rolls; in others, from driver's license lists) are called for jury duty, where they are questioned and either seated, excused for cause, or excused by a peremptory challenge by either side. Generally, challenge for cause involves jurors who have a relationship with a party or witness, have some personal experience that would impede their ability to be impartial, or are legally unable to sit. Peremptory challenges are limited in number and can be made by either side, for any or no reason; these are given to each side by rule or statute.[54] There has been some criticism of the use of peremptory challenges, for allowing private bias under the guise of fairness. Justice Sandra Day O'Connor commented in a dissent:

> The peremptory challenge "allow[s] parties," in this case *private* parties, to exclude potential jurors. It is the nature of a peremptory that its exercise is left wholly within the discretion of the litigant. . . . By allowing the litigant to strike jurors for even the most subtle of discerned biases, the peremptory challenge fosters both the perception and reality of an impartial jury. In both criminal and civil trials, the peremptory challenge is a mechanism for the exercise of *private* choice in the pursuit of fairness. The peremptory is, by design an enclave of private action in a government-managed proceeding.[55]

Racially biased use of peremptory challenges by the prosecution has been, and continues to be, a major source of unfair and often inaccurate jury verdicts.[56] There are lots of reasons for this, including structural racism as well as bias of the individual prosecutors, defense attorneys, and often judges.

I was representing a man named Edward Miller (not his real name), who was charged with a number of crimes, including the rape of a white woman. Edward, who was Black, was kind of unexceptional looking: balding, medium complexion and built, and about 5-foot-8. He certainly wasn't someone anyone would look twice at if they saw him walking down the street; he did not have an intimidating presence or affect— other than being Black, of course.

The issue in Edward's case was whether the complaining witness had made an accurate identification; in other words, was he the right guy? Because there was no physical evidence against Edward, no DNA or fingerprints, the whole case rose or fell on that identification.

"How do we let them know it ain't me?" Edward asked during a visit at the jail.

"That is a problem," I explained. "It is very difficult to prove a negative, especially without an alibi."

Edward had been arrested for this crime about three weeks after it happened, and he simply did not know where he was at the time, although he told me he was likely at home with his girlfriend. Even if he had been sure, being at home with your girlfriend isn't the kind of alibi that is persuasive; the easy prosecutorial response to that is to point out the lack of objective corroboration—after all, his girlfriend was biased, right?

"What do you mean?" he asked.

"Well, if the complaining witness gets up on the stand, tells this heartbreaking story of being raped and points at you as the guy who did it—and does so confidently—the jury is likely to take her word for it," I responded. "One thing that is very counterintuitive to jurors is that just because she might sound sure, doesn't mean she is accurate. In fact, sometimes the opposite is true, especially with crossracial identification."

Edward shrugged. "We all look alike . . . ," he muttered.

I smiled sadly. I knew what he meant, if not how it felt. "Edward, let me talk to you about identification and the role race plays in it. I am hoping the judge will let me put on an expert witness about this, but he doesn't have to, unfortunately."

At the time of Edward's case, judges were not obligated to allow eye-witness experts. In its 2016 decision in *People v. Lerma*, however, the Illinois Supreme Court made it clear that the rights to due process and a fair trial include the right to present witnesses on one's own behalf.[57] The court carefully noted the progression of jurisprudence on eyewitness experts:

> [W]e would like briefly to comment on the current state of jurisprudence concerning the admission of eyewitness expert testimony . . . which contrary to the trial court's belief, cannot possibly be dismissed as a mere "issue du jour." . . . [Recent decades] have seen a dramatic shift in the legal landscape, as expert testimony concerning the reliability of eyewitness testimony has moved from novel and uncertain to settled and widely accepted.[58]

The court went on to discuss multiple states across the country that have moved the needle with regard to acceptance of and the expectation of and need for eyewitness experts in the court room when appropriate. And finally, the court concluded, "[T]oday we are able to recognize that such research is well settled, well supported, and in appropriate cases a perfectly proper subject for expert testimony."[59] While Illinois made this change in 2016, the progression has occurred in nearly all states over the last thirty years. Today, nearly all states now allow the use of eyewitness experts at the discretion of the trial judge.[60]

But back to Edward: In the course of his trial, the judge was not obligated to allow it.

"Well then, he won't," Edward said.

I had to agree. Judge O'Halloran (also an alias) was a terrible judge from the defense perspective, and a not-very-subtle racist, to boot. He also didn't care for women or Jewish people, having called me a "Jew bitch" in chambers already. I couldn't prove it, though, as the only other witnesses to that outburst were prosecutors, who certainly would not have backed me up. I heard he laughed about it later, saying that he hadn't been sure I was a Jew before, but my reaction—stunned silence—told him I was. He was supposed to have laughed again and said, "I was sure about the bitch part, though."

I then explained the common misperceptions about eyewitness identification, especially in these circumstances.[61] I told Edward about the three stages of eyewitness memory: acquisition, retention, retrieval. Each stage is kind of self-explanatory: Acquisition occurs when the event happens, retention is the period between when the event happens and memory recollection occurs, and retrieval is when the individual pulls up the memory. The problem is that as soon as the acquisition stage is over, memory fades rapidly.[62] I explained that each of these stages allows for flaws to occur that ultimately affect perceptions and memories. Our brain is not like a video recorder; instead, as renowned memory scholar Dr. Elizabeth Loftus explained in 2013, memory works more like *Wikipedia*, where you can go in and edit your memories—and so can other people.[63]

Then I talked to Edward about the distortion that occurs during highly traumatic and emotional events. Even important and critical events are not immune from distortion. While an emotional event will be remembered better than a neutral one,[64] sometimes people relay memories of highly emotional and consequential events (like 9/11 or the JFK assassination) with a high level of detail and confidence, only to discover that their memories are actually inaccurate.[65]

I also told Edward that unless it is corroborated, there is just no way to tell whether a memory is true or false. If a person tells someone else that the van parked out front had a taillight out and a dent, this could be true, or this could be a reconstructed memory from having heard others comment about the car later or even from questioning that implied the taillight was out. And the phrasing of a question can make a difference as well. For example, a witness who is asked how fast the car was going when an accident occurred will often state a lower number than if they are asked how fast the car was going when they saw it crash into the other car. Further, research indicates that both false and true memories can feel the same—both can be described with great confidence and in great detail.[66]

Basically, I told Edward, eyewitnesses make mistakes.[67] And we know that these mistakes are the leading cause of wrongful convictions.[68] The Innocence Project has identified more than 365 individuals who have been exonerated by DNA evidence proving that they did not commit the crimes for which they were convicted, and this accounts for a combined total of over four thousand years in prison for crimes these wrongfully convicted individuals did not commit. While multiple factors can play into a wrongful conviction, the Innocence Project found that nearly 70 percent of these cases involved mistaken eyewitness testimony—and when a witness is white and the alleged perpetrator is not, the potential for error is higher.[69] And the average juror, like many working within the legal community, does not have this understanding of memory phenomena.[70]

I went on to tell Edward about conscious and unconscious bias. Conscious racism is just what it sounds like, and unfortunately it has become socially acceptable in our country again. Unconscious bias is hard to see in others and even harder to see ourselves.

Unconscious racism and biases often play a role in our everyday decisions.[71] Racial biases might cause us to "treat members of different racial groups disparately." Legally, and in the sciences, there are two terms used to describe type of bias: explicit and implicit. Explicit bias refers to the kinds of bias that people knowingly express and sometimes embrace. Implicit bias is not stated, it is more nuanced, and it is rarely acknowledged.

Implicit bias is often so subtle or ingrained that those who hold the bias are not aware of it.[72] Implicit bias is especially difficult to discuss because even when we are in touch with them, we are unlikely to admit to or address our own implicit racial biases. Biases can and do influence our interpretation of benign behavior, causing us to read identical behaviors differently based on the race of the actor. Moreover, studies have shown that we engage in "race loyalty," assuming the best in people who are of the same race as us because of our desire to see our race (and ourselves) in a positive light.[73]

This explanation (without citations) took the better part of an hour, with Edward asking questions and nodding as things made sense to him. After I was done, I looked at him expectantly; I figured he would have questions or at least a reaction to all of this information.

"So how are we going to fight all this?" he asked, not unreasonably.

"Well, we will try to do so with an expert, and with the way that I cross-examine the police as well as the complaining witness," I said. "But what is going to be absolutely crucial is our jury. It simply is not possible to speak reason to someone who has closed their ears, and so we have to try to find people who can listen." *Easier said than done*, I thought.

I explained to Edward that many, if not most, prosecutors used peremptory challenges in a racially biased way, to eliminate other Black jurors or folks they see as unduly sympathetic to civil rights. I explained how dangerous it would be for us if we ended up with an all-white jury and a homogenous one. I told him that the United States Supreme Court had tried to address this issue, but that it had not succeeded.

In *Batson v. Kentucky*, the United States Supreme Court held that when the defense believed that biased peremptory challenges were occurring, an objection would be made to the trial judge, and if the trial judge found that a prima facie case had been made, the prosecution would have to give race-neutral reasons for the exclusions. If the trial court accepted these explanations, the trial would continue. If not, a mistrial would be declared.[74] This procedure was supposed to fix the problem.

It hasn't exactly had that effect, however. Once defense counsel has made the objection and established a prima facie showing, prosecutorial tendering and judicial acceptance of "race-neutral" explanations that prove acceptable to reviewing courts has become nearly pro forma. For example, in *People v. Randall*, before reversing the case and remanding for a *Batson* violation, the Court observed:

> Having made these observations [about the function of a *Batson* challenge], we now consider the charade that has become the *Batson* process. The State may provide the trial court with a series of pat race-neutral reasons for exercise of peremptory challenges. Since reviewing courts examine only the record, we wonder if the reasons can be given without a smile. Surely, new prosecutors are given a manual, probably entitled, "Handy Race-Neutral Explanations" or "20 Time-Tested Race-Neutral

Explanations." It might include: too old, too young, divorced, "long, unkempt hair," free-lance writer, religion, social worker, renter, lack of family contact, attempting to make eye-contact with defendant, "lived in an area consisting predominantly of apartment complexes," single, over-educated, lack of maturity, improper demeanor, unemployed, improper attire, juror lived alone, misspelled place of employment, living with girl-friend, unemployed spouse, spouse employed as school teacher, employ-ment as part-time barber, friendship with city council member, failure to remove hat, lack of community ties, children same "age bracket" as defendant, deceased father and prospective juror's aunt receiving psychi-atric care. [Footnotes with citations to a case upholding these explanations have been omitted.] . . . Recent consideration of the *Batson* issue makes us wonder if the rule would be imposed only where the prosecutor states that he does not care to have an African-American on the jury. We are reminded of the musing of Justice Cardozo, "We are not to close our eyes as judges to what we must perceive as men."[75]

Of course, *Batson* is relevant only to the issue of exclusion of iden-tifiable groups from jury service; it has nothing to do with the far more pervasive and dangerous issue of racial bias *among* jurors. A jury that isn't diverse and doesn't have a variety of life experiences tends to fol-low authority, in this case the prosecution, which is often backed up by the judge.

Edward's prediction was correct regarding the judge's rulings; he denied us the option to call an expert on eyewitness identification, se-verely restricted our questioning of potential jurors (called voir dire), and consistently ruled with the prosecution's requests.

During jury selection, Judge O'Halloran asked the prospective jurors if any of them, or someone close to them, had been the victim of a crime. A white woman in her early fifties with a thin, tense smile raised her hand.

"Yes?" asked the judge.

"My daughter was raped by a Black man," she said. Then she stared at Edward. "They never caught him." At this point you might think, *Well of course the judge will excuse her for cause; obviously this hits too close to home for her.* You would be wrong. The judge followed up: "Well, ma'am, the fact that your daughter was raped by a Black man, and the defendant is a Black man charged with having raped a white woman"—he paused, swallowed, and appeared to lick his lips—"that doesn't mean you wouldn't be fair to the defendant, does it? You could be fair."

Nodding while staring at Edward, she responded, "Of course I can be fair."

When I asked to follow up with her, my request was denied, as was my request to have her removed for cause, so I had to use a peremptory challenge. I ran out of them pretty quickly, and we ended up with an all-white jury with one elderly Black man as the second alternate.

However, often the use of race as a proxy isn't so obvious. For example, during jury selection in another case, I was discussing the relative veracity of police versus other witnesses. One of the potential jurors, a Black woman, expressed that not only did she not give police more credibility (which jurors often do), she gave them less. When I asked if she believed she could be fair to both sides, she said yes, but I knew the prosecution would excuse her. We discussed other issues for a bit, and it was clear that she was educated, with a master's in public policy as I recall, and very smart and savvy. So when, as expected, the prosecution excused her, she stood up and asked the judge if she could say something. Startled, he said she could, and she looked right at the prosecutors and asked them a question: "Why is it that the prosecution is so frightened of having any educated Black person on this jury?"

She then named three Black potential jurors that she had watched be excused before her. No one responded.

"That's what I thought," she said to the prosecutors, then she nodded at me and walked out.

I wish I could tell you that we won the case anyway, but we did not. I did not know then, and do not know now, if Edward committed the crime, but I do know that racism played a big part in his conviction—and the system allowed and in fact encouraged it to.

After the guilty verdict, I went back in the lockup to express my regret and to try to be supportive. Edward looked at me sadly. "You warned me," he said. "I wish it weren't so, but"—he paused—"thanks for not pretending."

We all have to stop pretending.

Racism impacts the criminal justice system, and when we focus on "the system" we need to remember that the system is made up of individuals who are impacted in very real ways. We speak about the system, but we need to remember the individuals like Edward. From stops and arrests to verdicts and sentences, the impact of racial bias is not only on a system as a whole, played out through statistics. It is much more than that: Lives of the accused and the accusers are affected, as are their families, friends, and communities. Each statistic is represented by individuals who, along with their loved ones, feel the brunt of this bias.

The fact that there are harsher sentences for Black and brown people is not simply a comparison of Black and brown people to white people. It is a comparison of a man like Edward, who is forced to sit in prison, to a different man, a White man, who gets off with probation or who is possibly never arrested in the first place. Comparing police incidents is not just a numbers game; it is the knowledge that police officers' bias may cause them to kill a Black person but gently arrest (and even buy Burger King for!)[76] a white person. And then there is bias among jurors—the individuals who are literally in control of the accused's future life or lack thereof. All along the way, bias informs their decision making, their evaluation of the facts, and their ability to deliver a fair verdict.

So what could an Office of the Defender General of the United States do about the issue of racial bias, narrowing our focus for right now just to jury selection? Well, it could make racially biased behavior personally costly to the lawyers who engage in it, perhaps subjecting them to discipline or relieving them from their immunity in a civil suit. It could create training and best practices for the defense. It could collaborate with the Department of Justice and the judicial college to do the same for prosecutors and judges.

The Defender General could be a voice and a presence to confront racial injustice in our system. The United States needs a Defender General.

4

The Inequality Tax

The Economic Case for Criminal Justice Reform

It is nearly a cliché to say that you get what you pay for, but it is true, especially in the criminal justice arena. If we, as a society, want punishment above all else, the criminal justice system will not change. There will be no change in criminal acts and no societal improvement. Instead, we will continue to build, maintain, and grow an incarcerated class. We will also maintain a class of people who arrest people, process them, investigate them, prosecute them, and guard them once they are in jail and prison.

Even with great strides made at identifying and assessing problems within the criminal justice system, we end up tinkering at the edges of problems and never getting to the center. How can we have a system we can trust when the people it purports to serve—all the people—are not a part of it and are not listened to? So long as prosecutors make poor and politically motivated charging decisions—and are allowed, even encouraged, to do so—nothing will change.

As Jonathan Rapping notes in his book *Gideon's Promise*, without culture change, without an emphasis on the human endeavor that is the search for justice, that which is barely acknowledged, there will be no lasting change.[1] So long as success in policing is gauged by arrest numbers and not communities that feel they can turn to the police for help, there will be no culture change and no real change. So long as prosecutors simply tout their conviction rates, there will be no change. So long as politicians are judged on how "tough on crime"—or, to make it more palatable, "committed to safety"—they claim to be, there will be no change. So long as judges are produced from a prosecutor pipeline, incentivized by reelection cycles, and hamstrung by mandatory minimums, there will be no change. So long as all these cycles continue, no amount of grant funding or Marshall Projects or Innocence Projects will actually change the criminal justice system. Don't get me wrong—these efforts are extremely important and should be built upon and expanded as much as possible. But they simply will not solve the problems we face within the criminal justice system.

For many, discussions of the need for reform need not be on social, moral, or humanitarian grounds. Instead, most people are interested in reform only as it will practically affect them. However, most citizens want to feel safe, and they also want to pay less in taxes. The repeal of the death penalty in Illinois is a case in point. Many people wanted to see the death penalty go for moral and humanitarian reasons; for others, because of the state's despicable record of convicting and sentencing to death the wrong person altogether (before the death penalty's end, Illinois executed twelve and exonerated nineteen); and for still others, it was the economic argument that moved them, and ultimately moved the legislature to take action. As Jeremy Schroeder, then the executive director of the Illinois Coalition to Abolish the Death Penalty, wrote:

> The death penalty needs to be abolished in Illinois because it is cost-prohibitive. We need to use our scarce resources to make sure we are smart on crime by investing in personal and resources that make our communities safer and also care for victims of crime. . . . Death penalty cases are clearly more expensive at every stage of the judicial process than similar non-death cases. Everything that is needed for an ordinary trial is needed for a death penalty case, only more so. . . . Many other states have looked at the costs of their death row and have found it to be much more expensive than the alternatives.[2]

Thus an unusual coalition was formed: Victims' rights groups, who wanted funding spent on their needs, not death penalty trials; fiscal conservatives, who didn't think that Illinois got much "bang for its buck"; and those of us who wanted the death penalty gone for moral, religious, or philosophical reasons all joined together.[3]

It is easier to see the cost of "expensive" prosecutions like death penalty cases than it is to see where decisions by prosecutors, police, and, to some extent, judges, affect what we spend and where we spend it—and how shortsightedly we do both. While there are some cases where there is a public outcry to charge someone—anyone, really—and pressure to make the decision to charge and what to charge rapidly, that is not true with most cases. The default position of most prosecutors is to charge the largest possible number of charges, which often results in one act being charged under dozens of legal theories, as well as those that carry the most severe penalties, even if it is clear (or later becomes clear) that it is overcharging—deliberately charging multiple counts, with knowledge that most charges will fall away as proceedings begin. Overcharging is not specifically prohibited by lawyers' rules of professional conduct and is is used as a technique for future plea bargaining.[4]

Overcharging forces individuals into pleas because the risk is just too great. If faced with the death penalty or life without parole, a plea to a lesser charge—and therefore, less time—becomes appealing. Even innocent people "choose" the plea, as the risk of going to trial is so astronomical.[5]

In many situations, there is a price paid by the system, the accused, and their families as a result of thoughtless overcharging and because of a powerful force called inertia. It is difficult for someone—especially someone with as much power as the prosecution—to reconsider a decision that has already been made, even if it was made without much thought.

Take the case of Tess Andrews (not her real name). It wasn't hard to see Tess Andrews's pain. It was, quite literally, stamped on her face. When the preliminary hearing judge assigned me to represent her, I stepped up to the bench and glanced at her. She was petite, maybe 5-foot-4, thin but solid, and looked to be in her fifties but was actually only forty-two. She was African American, with medium complexion and short hair that looked like she had been in jail for a while—which she had. But what caught my attention was her face: the round, one-inch burn on her left cheek, maybe two inches below her eye, that I would later learn happened when Carson Andrews (also not his real name) extinguished a cigar there; the scar above her right eyebrow that she told the hospital had come from a fall; and her uneven jaw, as most of her teeth on the left side had been knocked out from another "fall."

Tess was charged with first-degree murder in Carson's death. In Illinois, defendants can be so charged without premeditation of any kind—if they act knowingly and know that their actions are likely to cause great bodily harm or death, and someone does in fact die because their actions, that is first-degree murder. The bond court judge had set a no-bail order based on the charges. Looking at Tess more closely, I could see bandages on her left arm and one that appeared to be sticking out of her jail-issue orange top. Just looking at her I could tell there was self-defense in this case, that she was a battered woman. *First-degree murder?* I thought to myself. *Isn't this obviously not that?*

The prosecution wasn't ready to do a preliminary hearing, and I knew they wouldn't hold one anyway. They would go straight to the grand jury—where neither Tess nor I could be present—to get charges approved, they would have an officer testify to the summary of the case, and she would be indicted, undoubtedly by the next court date. I asked the judge for a reduction in bond, as Tess had only a minimal criminal record, mostly for drunk and disorderly charges and most of which were dropped. She had a teenage daughter and other family, so she had ties to the community. But the judge wouldn't lower her bond, and frankly, it seemed unlikely that her family would be able to post much in any case—certainly not the thousands of dollars it would take to bond someone out on this charge. Yes, there is a presumption of innocence, but judges in most states, including Illinois, run for election. No one wants to be the judge who released someone charged with a serious offense who does something violent while on bond. Tess was going to be in custody until her trial.

I gave her my card and told her I would be over to the women's division to see her the following day.

As I went into the women's division of the jail, I found myself feeling extra uneasy, as I often I did around other women who were locked up. It felt too close to home, I imagine. I went into the interview room and waited for the guards to bring Tess Andrews down. I stood when she entered and reintroduced myself. She was looking at the floor.

"Miss Andrews?" I asked. "Are you doing okay, as much as that is possible, in here?" She shrugged, so I tried again: "Miss Andrews, do you remember who I am? Why I am here?"

"There's no point," she said quietly. "I stabbed him. He's dead. I am going to jail." She said all this with almost no affect at all. Her expression was dull, her voice monotone, and her attitude hopeless.

"That isn't exactly true," I replied. "It looks to me, just looking at you, that you were injured too, and it is likely that we can show you were acting in self-defense."

"Yeah. No one cares. Me an' Carson, we drank, we fought, and this was bound to happen."

"What do you mean?"

"He was gonna kill me or I was gonna kill him." I heard just a little emotion. "I can't stand it." I waited. "I shoulda left. I shoulda left."

We talked some more, and she gave me the names of people who knew about the relationship and signed some releases so I could get her medical records.

As we investigated the case, my suspicions about their marriage proved true. Police had been called to their tiny apartment many times. Tess had been hospitalized a number of times as well, and we gathered those records and spoke to doctors and nurses, many of whom told us they didn't believe for a minute that Tess had fallen. Both Tess and Carson drank a good deal, as she had told me, and the autopsy report showed that Carson had cirrhosis of the liver, albeit in early stages, and had a blood alcohol level of 2.7—nearly three times the legal limit—at the time of his death.

Tess's health wasn't good either. She had high blood pressure and stomach problems. Months passed as I worked on the case, and I developed a pretty good relationship with her. She began to trust me, to tell me about the beatings and the time he had stabbed her in front of their daughter. That was when Tess asked her mom to take Tess's daughter in. "She don't need to see no stuff like that," she told me.

One Thursday afternoon, I got a collect call from her from the jail. That was unusual; she seldom called. "Hey Tess," I said after pressing all the buttons needed to accept the call. "Miss Lyon," she said, "I don't feel so good."

That wasn't like her either; she didn't complain much. In fact, in my view, she didn't complain *enough*. When I asked her what was wrong, she said she had a terrible headache and was dizzy, and that she had fallen earlier. She had asked to go to medical, but no one had come, so she was wondering if I could help.

I called over to the watch commander, explained the situation, and asked that she be taken to Cermak Hospital, the medical wing for Cook County Jail. I was told someone would go get her. I thanked her and then turned to some other work.

But no one brought her to medical, so when the aneurysm in her brain burst, they took her to the hospital in a coma. She was then transported to Cook County Hospital, still in a coma. To reduce the swelling in her brain, doctors put a shunt in, along with a trach in her throat so she could breathe. But she was deemed dangerous because she was charged with first-degree murder, so they shackled her to the bed and put a guard outside her door. Neither her mother nor her daughter were allowed to visit her. I went to court and got a court order allowing the visits.

Then I had to have a hearing to prove there was no reason to shackle her to the bed, and get a court order for that. That hearing was Kafkaesque, with the prosecution alleging that she was a murderer and might run off—with a shunt in her brain and a trach in her throat. I got the order, but it took several days of serving it to everyone and their brother to get the shackles taken off. Then we held a fitness hearing.

Obviously, since she was in a coma, Tess wasn't fit for trial. Under the law, if it could be anticipated, medically, that she would become fit within a year, the court would wait for that, but if not, then we had to hold a discharge hearing so that she would either be found "guilty" or "not guilty." If guilty, she could be held for five years. So I ended up trying the case with an empty chair by my side, with both Tess's daughter and her mother listening. The judge took a continuance for his ruling. Two days before we were to come back to court, Tess died.

If there had been a good investigation in the first place—if the police had just looked up Carson's criminal history—they would have seen he had been violent toward her. If they had looked at Tess's wounds from the day Carson was killed—if they had looked at her *face*—they would have known this was a battered woman who had acted in self-defense. The most she should have been charged with was manslaughter, and if she had, she would have been released on bond. When she got that headache, she could have gone to the doctor or an ER. I spoke to her primary doctor when I learned of her death. He told me the aneurysm had been operable, that if she had been brought to the hospital an hour or two before she was, she would have lived.

But no one saw her. Not the police, not the prosecutor, not the judge who refused to set bail. She was just another Black woman who stabbed her man. So who cares?

Another "cost" that is rarely discussed is the health and life costs associated with being incarcerated. Most inmates come out of prison with premature health conditions due to a lack of sufficient healthcare and suffer enormous mental health challenges—and this is if they get out at all. Many sit in prison for the remainder of their life and some die at the hands of the prison system.[6]

A Defender General could influence charging decisions and help to institutionalize the review of charging decisions before trial. In the US Attorney's manual, there is already precedent that gives the defense the opportunity to "make the case" against the prosecution of a death penalty case.[7] The process is complex, but a Defender General could help to develop best practices to ensure there is a process for reconsidering what charges are appropriate.

Another hidden cost of the system is its errors.[8] In chapter 3, I discussed—and critiqued—the shield of absolute immunity, molded over more than a century into something that completely contradicts its original intent.[9] One of the most egregious forms of prosecutorial misconduct that is ultimately protected by this immunity involves what is called a *Brady* violation.[10] A *Brady* violation occurs when a prosecutor, or anyone working in support of the state's case, withholds exculpatory evidence from the defense.[11] In other words, if the police, crime lab, prosecutors, or anyone else working with the prosecution know anything that might show the accused is innocent or deserves a lesser punishment, they have to provide it to the defense. This includes evidence that might lead to something good for the defense if it is investigated. Unfortunately, this duty is more often observed in the breach. For example, during an investigation of one death penalty case, Jamie Kunz and I canvased the neighborhood in which the shootings occurred. We found a lady whose picture window overlooked the spot where the shooting occurred and found out that she was an eyewitness and had been taken to see a lineup (which our client was in) and had not made an identification. We had not been told of this lineup, nor the name of this witness. We certainly should have been, since the fact that an eyewitness did not identify our client was evidence in his favor.

The United States Supreme Court summarized this due process violation in 1963,[12] holding in *Brady v. Maryland* that "suppression by the prosecution of evidence favorable to an accused upon request violates due process where the evidence is material either to guilt or to punishment, irrespective of the good faith or bad faith of the prosecution."[13] Further, the Court in *Brady* named the injustice that can occur when the prosecutor is calling all the shots:

A prosecution that withholds evidence on demand of an accused which, if made available, would tend to exculpate him or reduce the penalty helps shape a trial that bears heavily on the defendant. That casts the prosecutor in the role of an architect of a proceeding that does not comport with standards of justice.[14]

A *Brady* violation occurs if the prosecution suppresses evidence that is deemed favorable to the defense and that evidence is relevant and significant to the facts of the case.[15] This leaves entirely too much decision-making power in the hands of prosecutors, as discussed above with the example of the unreported lineup.[16]

The other problem is that whether or not something is favorable to the accused is a value judgement, requiring that prosecutors make decisions about whether a particular piece of evidence would be considered valuable to the defense.[17] This asks the prosecutors to decide what is and is not important for the defense to know about. Maurice Possley, a journalist with prosecutorial expertise, and Thomas Sullivan, who has practiced law for more than sixty years, made a particularly keen analogy that illustrates the problematic discretion afforded to prosecutors: "Imagine a professional sporting event in which one of the contestants is permitted to make the close calls—whether it was a ball or strike, whether the tennis ball was in or out, whether the tackle was offside, etc.—without oversight by an independent umpire."[18] The prosecutors charged with making tough calls on the use of evidence call their own balls and strikes, oftentimes prioritizing a win over engaging fairly with the system.

Prosecutors cannot know every investigative puzzle piece defense attorneys may have cultivated,[19] leaving them guessing as to whether something should be considered favorable or not. Defense attorneys are much better poised to determine what evidence will best support their client.[20]

When prosecutors withhold exculpatory evidence, justice is not served.[21] The Court further tailored the rules in subsequent cases,[22] but prosecutors still have broad discretion[23] and are often challenged to act within the confines of competing values: pursuing a conviction and appropriate outcomes for a criminal defendant they may honestly believe is guilty while evaluating ethical considerations and less tangible notions regarding "fair play."[24] So even though the United States Supreme Court has spoken on this, first in *Brady* and many times over the years, there are still too many violations of the law, the most egregious, of course, being those that result in wrongful convictions.

Wrongful convictions ruin the lives of innocent individuals, many of whom will never regain their freedom.[25] Rather, they are taken from their families and experience detrimental effects on their physical and mental health.[26] Wrongful convictions also allow individuals who actually commit crimes to remain free, causing safety risks to communities and society as a whole.[27] When the wrong individual sits in prison, the actual perpetrator of a crime is free to commit additional crimes.[28] This injustice creates substantial negative impacts for victims and victims' families, in particular those who begin to understand that the person in prison is not the person who harmed them or their loved one.[29]

There are also high taxpayer costs incurred when a person is wrongfully convicted.[30] The courts must administer a trial (and often multiple resulting appellate proceedings) for an innocent person.[31] Offices of prosecution and public defense incur costs during these proceedings.[32] Wrongful convictions also incur incarceration costs.[33] Federally, the cost for incarcerating one inmate in fiscal year 2018 was between $34,000 and $38,000, depending on the facility.[34] Costs are similar in state prisons.[35] When individuals are wrongfully convicted, taxpayers pay court and prison costs for individuals who do not belong there.[36] So while there is an outcry from many that criminals need to be locked away, those same people would not be happy to know they are paying for folks to be in prison who should not be there, while the actual people who committed the crimes are still on the streets.

Additionally, there is almost no accountability for prosecutors when these violations occur. For one, in appellate processes, courts will only overturn and/or vacate on a *Brady* violation if the appellant can meet a very high bar, showing all three elements of the rule: suppression, favorability, and materiality.[37] While suppression and favorability can be proven, the materiality requirement demands there be a reasonable probability that the evidence would have changed the outcome of the case.[38]

When a judge finds that a violation has occurred, the violation leads to an overturned conviction only if the defendant can prove that he or she suffered identifiable prejudice based on the *Brady* violation.[39] And judges often protect prosecutors as much as they can. Even when judges discuss *Brady* violations within appellate opinions, they often go out of their way to avoid identifying prosecutors who are implicated in those violations.[40] For example, the Florida Supreme Court and California Supreme Court both heard cases in the late 1990s with findings of serious prosecutorial misconduct. In both sets of circumstances, lower courts had already admonished bad behavior when authoring appellate decisions, but always with the overt decision to use "Assistant United States Attorney" (or AUSA) in their written decisions instead of personally naming the prosecutorial offender.[41] In California, the prosecutor engaged in misconduct during a death penalty case many years after she was first admonished (but never by name) within appellate decisions.[42] The California Supreme Court became aware of the two prior admonishing decisions only because of research conducted and submitted by the appellant's attorneys.[43] In both the California and the Florida examples, the prosecutors resigned, which prevented future misconduct from occurring.[44] While these examples are by no means singular,[45] it is unusual for prosecutors to be named in appellate decisions.[46] Thus, even when an appellant overcomes *Brady*, it is not likely that the prosecutor who committed the violation will be held accountable by way of the appellate process.[47]

And as discussed in chapter 2, the United States Supreme Court held in *Connick v. Thompson* that "plaintiffs who seek to impose liability on local governments under § 1983 must prove that 'action pursuant to official municipal policy' caused their injury."[48] So offices responsible for prosecution are left free to do as they choose, and wrongly convicted individuals have almost no successful recourse.

How about holding a prosecutor accountable by way of a criminal process? Wait a minute, wait a minute—you mean I am actually suggesting that a prosecutor be charged with a crime? Now I am really delving into uncharted territory. Prosecutions of prosecutors for misconduct are nearly nonexistent.[49] At the federal level, prosecutors can be criminally prosecuted for violating constitutional protections under 18 U.S.C. § 242.[50] However, this avenue proves more theoretical than practical and is rarely used.[51]

A comprehensive report put out by the National Registry of Exonerations cites only two known prosecutions at the state level.[52] In both cases, the prosecutors who became the defendants received nominal sentences.[53] In 2007, Michael Nifong, the former District Attorney of Durham County, North Carolina, was convicted of criminal contempt for concealing exculpatory evidence in a prosecution of three members of the Duke University Lacrosse team who were falsely accused of rape.[54] Nifong spent one day in jail.[55] The attention this case received resulted in an additional exoneration for someone previously tried by Nifong in 1991.[56] And in 2013, former Williamson County, Texas, District Attorney Ken Anderson was convicted of contempt after concealing exculpatory evidence that would have prevented a wrongful conviction for a man who spent twenty-four years in prison before his exoneration.[57] Anderson spent four days in jail. Although Nifong and Anderson spent only five days in jail between them, they were both eventually disbarred and lost their jobs.[58] As of this writing, the National Registry of Exonerations names these two as "the only two American prosecutors who have ever been convicted of criminal contempt for lying in court."[59]

The number of criminal prosecutions of prosecutors is likely so low due to a societal perception that criminal liability is too harsh for someone who made a technical error in the course of their demanding and stressful work.[60] The legal community may prefer alternate avenues of accountability, reserving criminal proceedings for those practice errors considered most egregious.[61] So a prosecutor is free to charge nearly whenever he wants, even if he is hiding evidence and calling all the shots—perhaps leading to wrongful convictions and perhaps putting away individuals who did not commit a crime—and all of this seems to be accepted as the norm. But the misconduct the prosecutor engages in to get that conviction? There is not really any avenue of repercussion for that misconduct at all.

This sort of prosecutorial misconduct is a serious issue, playing a role in nearly every wrongful conviction, and yet is not addressed in any systematic or systemic way. An Office of the Defender General could address these sorts of violations by, for example, providing funding and expertise to create a database of "repeat offenders" so that reviewing courts might know with whom they are dealing, or by holding trainings of prosecutors by defense lawyers on how to identify evidence that is favorable to the defense.

There are many other ways in which the system costs us all. When we spend more on prisons than schools and impoverish families who have to buy "commissary" for their loved ones who are incarcerated, thus ensuring even more poverty, we are making a choice. Governments make fiscal choices that hurt our society, and there is no one to say,

"Stop." For example, according to the Vera Institute of Justice, Kentucky jails and county governments made $9.6 million off payments for phone calls and other services in their jails during the 2020 fiscal year and nearly $900,000 in telecom contract "signing bonuses" since 2010.[62] And we are making an expensive choice—when an entire industry profits from incarceration of individuals and the impact on their families—and that choice does not help us as a society.

This plays out in a few ways. For example, another cost consideration is how we, as a society, are choosing to spend our resources. A look at government expenditures on education compared to spending on inmates paints a poignant picture.[63] According to the US Census Bureau and the Vera Institute, there is not a single state for which more money is spent on education than it is spent on inmates.[64]

Another example: there is an entire privatized industry around prisons.[65] With more than 2.1 million people in US prisons as of 2018, it only makes sense that some of them would be housed privately through contracts from the US government. Private prisons provide the facilities, the staff, the food, everything.[66] And while public prisons do not have the end goal of making a profit, private prisons do.[67] Corporations enter contracts with the government, and payment is often based on the number of prisoners housed.[68] See how this makes sense? People's lives, their guilt and innocence, become a means to make money. And, as Sean Bryant notes, "[I]f prison was 100% effective [in rehabilitating prisoners], the private prisons would be working themselves out of business. This makes one wonder: is prison supposed to rehabilitate the individual, or is it supposed to earn money? If the goal is to earn money, then a high prison population is the end goal."[69]

Every study tells us that incarcerated individuals who maintain close contact with family and friends have a far lower recidivation rate than those who do not. If our interest is in reformation and positive outcomes, shouldn't we encourage this contact? Instead of it costing a single mother upward of $200 a month to talk to her husband, why isn't that something that we simply underwrite?[70] Currently, there is no one to raise these issues in a sustained and centralized way, but a Defender General could.

These are examples of individual costs. But our local and state governments are incurring costs too. Which means—you guessed it!—taxpayers are incurring costs.

While we have discussed the cost to incarcerate someone federally, we have not yet discussed jail costs. Jails house people in a constant holding pattern: waiting for arraignment, waiting for trial, waiting for sentencing, waiting to be transferred to prison after sentencing, back to jail while waiting for their appeal. Jails are supposed to be temporary holding spaces, but they are anything but. Yet the United States spends more money on jails in a year than most might imagine. For example, as of the end of 2017, costs for jails and other local corrections had risen sixfold when compared to 1977.[71] The average cost of keeping a person in jail was about $34,000.[72] And again, this is just for the holding place. Further, even with crime and jail admission falling, jail costs are not letting up. A near 20 percent decrease in crime and jail admission between 2007 and the end of 2017 had not reduced spending at all.[73]

Jail and Corrections Expenditures, Local Government (In Billions)

Figure 4.1. Jail Costs. Corrections costs continue to rise. *Graph created by E. Kate Cohn. Data Source: Pew Charitable Trust and U.S. Census Bureau: https://www .pewtrusts.org/en/research-and-analysis/issue-briefs/2021/01/local-spending -on-jails-tops-$25-billion-in-latest-nationwide-data.*

While there are great costs to local governments associated with jails, there are economic incentives for governments and government actors to lock people up as well. Local sheriff's offices are an often overlooked source of this incentive. Mass incarceration is a machine, and it has many levers of power.[74] There are many people and entities with their hand on the levers, including legislators, police, prosecutors, judges, prison officials, and probation and parole officials. And as it turns out, even though we think of jail as the in-between time, the holding pattern place, the temporary stopover between arrest and criminal proceedings, jailers have quite a heavy hand on the levers of power as well.[75] Sheriffs, particularly in rural areas, exert an enormous amount of power and authority that dictates many individuals' freedom—or lack thereof.[76] Sheriffs decide when to build new jails. They decide if and when to release people. And they manage a supply-and-demand landscape—or should we call it a bedscape?[77] Sheriffs also shape the system politically, fundraising for jail projects, convincing voters to fund them, and brokering with commissioners to raise court fees to exorbitant levels, using the empty promise that those in the system should be on the hook financially so that the system "pays for itself."[78]

If a Defender General presented information to appellate courts with amicus (friend of the court) briefs, in a consolidated and concise manner that makes these costs visible, perhaps the economic incentives that drive incarceration would be more visible. The Defender General could assist local litigants regarding their use of law enforcement powers to fundraise. The United States needs a Defender General.

5

The War on Us

Laws That Caused Mass Incarceration

Defense attorneys learn to be wary of new laws based on their names. If a law has a name like the Antiterrorism and Effective Death Penalty Act of 1996,[1] you know nothing good will be contained in it. The title is a marketing ploy—who could possibly be against an antiterrorism bill? And if you are a supporter of the death penalty, how could you be against it being "effective"? The name is more than a clue; it is a clear signal that this law is going to crunch some accused's rights, access to courts, or both. As discussed in the first chapter, this is one of the many laws on the books designed to keep our clients out of the courtroom—except to plead guilty, of course—or to make it so difficult to get there, that you can spend literally years litigating whether or not you can litigate in the first place.

Another law that sounds like it is a good thing but has become a tool of overincarceration is RICO, a statute that applies to a wide range of conduct and contains abstract terms not easily correlated with everyday experience.

What is RICO, you may ask? The Racketeer Influenced and Corrupt Organizations (RICO) Act is a federal act that was enacted in 1970 and adopted by most states shortly thereafter. RICO prohibits four specific types of conduct: "(1) investing proceeds from a pattern of racketeering activity in an enterprise, (2) acquiring or maintaining control over an enterprise through a pattern of racketeering activity, (3) conducting or participating in the affairs of an enterprise through a pattern of racketeering activity, and (4) conspiring to do any of these types of conduct."[2]

RICO is a complex and unique statute, and it is one of the only US statutes that specifies both a criminal offense and a civil cause of action.[3] This means it may either be prosecuted federally or brought by private individuals as a civil claim.[4] And RICO is a statute that carries stiff penalties, in terms of both prison time and fines. The elements of RICO remain the same, whether tried criminally or civilly, but of course the burden of proof is different: In civil cases, the burden is a preponderance of evidence, while in criminal cases, it is guilt beyond a reasonable doubt.[5] Further, "RICO contains three terms of art: (1) 'racketeering activity,' (2) 'pattern' of racketeering activity, and (3) 'enterprise.'"[6]

So what is racketeering as it relates to the type of criminal cases discussed so far? It can include murder, kidnapping, and robbery, as well as a plethora of white-collar crimes.[7] In addition, the individual must be caught up in a pattern of behavior or actions;[8] for instance, gang activity. But a pattern can also be established with two similar actions that occur within a ten-year period.[9] Two similar actions seems a little low to be declared a pattern, but even if it is enough, there should be some modicum of proof beyond that of mere similarity. And then there is enterprise, defined as "any individual, partnership, corporation, association, or other legal entity, and any union or group of individuals associated in fact although not a legal entity."[10]

And you still might be asking, what does RICO have to do with these types of crimes? Truly, the bill was meant to go after organized crime—in particular, the Mafia—because of its influence both economically and politically. In the 1980s, likely because of the hysteria surrounding the crack cocaine "epidemic" and the so-called War on Drugs, the Department of Justice began to expand its use of RICO to include gangs.[11] This allowed prosecutors to take advantage of the RICO law to further stigmatize and criminalize using the many tools that RICO provides. The prosecution, both in federal court and in state courts as states began to adopt their own versions of RICO, focused on the enterprise, and thus made every member responsible for the actions of every other member, subjecting them to far more severe sentences. Wielding this weapon, prosecutors could be assured of turning members of the alleged gang, who were anxious to avoid the risk of a huge sentence.

One of the predicate acts that can turn a case into a far more serious (in terms of sentencing consequences) and more easily prosecuted

RICO offense is selling drugs. If two or more people in a neighborhood work together to sell drugs, they can be called an enterprise and prosecuted under RICO, making them eligible for far more time in prison than the offenses by themselves would. And RICO is not only a federal crime; most states also have similar laws. One of the challenging aspects to defending is that whenever a conspiracy is charged, hearsay that would normally be excluded is admissible as long as the statement is "in furtherance" of the conspiracy.

People respond with disbelief when I explain this to them. Take, for example, my client Alberto Jimenez (not his real name). Alberto was a soft-spoken young man who had a job as a dispatcher for a trucking company. He lived in the Wicker Park neighborhood in Chicago, and he had a girlfriend from Minnesota. I was sure that he had used and likely sold cocaine, but nothing about him indicated anything like the lifestyle one associates with a large-scale drug dealer. The girlfriend was the problem.

Alberto Jimenez was charged with a drug conspiracy, primarily with providing cocaine to a seller in Minnesota. That seller, Amy Pearson, learned the trade from her former boyfriend, Alex Dominguez, and when he died, she took over.

She had to find suppliers, and she found Alberto, my client, through an acquaintance of Alex who recommended him. She involved her entire family in the growing business, including her parents and her sister, and even her brother—who was a police officer—and would do favors like run license plates for the business.

Once charges were filed against Alberto, the central figure in this criminal case was government witness Amy Pearson. Although Amy's plea agreement was for truthful testimony, she had a history of lying in court, using a variety of other names in connection with numerous arrests in Chicago, Las Vegas, and Los Angeles.

What many people do not realize is that truth is the eye of the prosecutor. In other words, if the cooperator has given a statement to the prosecution that they believe and decide to use as evidence in a criminal prosecution, all that the witness need do to avoid the truth problem is to be consistent with their prior statements to law enforcement. Juries may think that there is some truth monitor in the courtroom that will act should the witness lie, but there is not. It is law enforcement alone—usually the prosecutors trying the case—who make the determination. It was with this knowledge that I looked at the discovery against my client.

After Alex died and Amy tried to take over his business, Alex's suppliers were all arrested and sent to prison. Amy was determined to maintain the possessions she had acquired and enjoyed before Alex's death, including a home in Schaumburg, a Camaro, a Ford Bronco, a family farm, snowmobiles, four-wheelers, Caribbean cruises, family vacations to Florida, duffel bags filled with gold jewelry, a diamond Rolex watch, and her prized possession: a yellow Corvette. So Amy began her own distribution business after meeting with Alberto, and sometime after that the two developed a personal relationship. It is during this time, she said, that she began making regular runs to Minnesota: taking a kilogram, selling it, and returning to Chicago. She said she took an average of two kilograms to Minnesota once a week.

Alberto was arrested after her agreement had been ironed out. Other than what Amy had to say, the only indication that Alberto had anything to do with cocaine was the less than 30 grams found in his sock drawer. In other words, Alberto had been found with only a user's amount.

Nonetheless, with her testimony that there were a lot of drugs, I explained to Alberto, the government could convict him of supplying drugs or selling them without *any* actual drugs being introduced into evidence.

"What?" Alberto exclaimed. Alberto was a handsome young man, and managed, despite being in jail, to always look well-groomed. I sighed. Explaining this to someone charged was complicated, not in the least because I found the law so unfair myself. Alberto was essentially the one left holding the bag, even though there was nothing in it except words.

"I know, I know," I said. "The corroboration they will have to support Amy's story will be through agents who watched her make sales in Minnesota and the paraphernalia that she had at her house when she was arrested: scales, bags, that sort of thing." I paused. "They have cocaine residue on some of that stuff, and a tiny bit of heroin in one of the bags." They also had the drugs—small amounts—from two buyers who would testify against Amy, and had turned her driver, who would say that it was at least two kilos of cocaine (primarily) a week, for months. That's why Amy needed to "give" the prosecution something—to avoid the kind of time mandated by the sentencing guidelines.

At the time of Alberto's case, the guidelines were no longer manda-tory (after thirty years of sentencing-related litigation), but the major charges had mandatory minimums that were (and are) extraordinarily draconian, leaving a trial judge very little room, sometimes no room, to fashion a sentence based on the offense and the offender. The guidelines were promulgated as a response to some wildly disparate sentencing seen in various federal courts, but, as is often the case, they did not fix what was broken and instead just made it worse. Had there been a Defender General to weigh in on this idea, perhaps the RICO statute would not have been as terrible, and it wouldn't have taken thirty years of terribly inapposite sentences to get any relief. For example, the disparity between sentencing for crack cocaine (used more often by minorities) and cocaine in powder form (used more often by whites) shows how easily these guidelines can result in inequitable sentences based on prejudice rather than evidence, and, in this case, have a ra-cially disparate impact.[12]

And while the guidelines are now only advisory, they still carry great weight and thus leave any sentence with which the government disagrees subject to appeal. The power is in what is charged, and it is a big hammer over the head of someone charged in federal court. So what happened to make those guidelines advisory only? Because of the disparate sentences that treated snitches and those who contested guilt so differently, many appeals worked their way through the courts. Why, for example, should Amy get seven and a half years while Alberto, if he could not or would not get a cooperator's deal, be subject to a manda-tory minimum of thirty years?

The Supreme Court began to look at these issues, starting with its January 12, 2005, ruling that its Sixth Amendment holding in *Blakely v. Washington*[13] and *Apprendi v. New Jersey*[14] applies to the Federal Sentencing Guidelines.[15] Given the mandatory nature of the sentencing guidelines, the Court found no relevant distinction between the sentence imposed pursuant to the Washington statutes in *Blakely* and the sentences imposed pursuant to the Federal Sentencing Guidelines in the cases be-fore the Court.[16] Accordingly, reaffirming its holding in *Apprendi*, the Court concluded that "[a]ny fact (other than a prior conviction) which is necessary to support a sentence exceeding the maximum authorized by the facts established by a plea of guilty or a jury verdict must be admitted by the defendant or proved to a jury beyond a reasonable doubt."[17] In other words, Alberto's case now would require a jury to find, beyond a reasonable doubt, that he had possessed the amount of drugs indicated—it could no longer be addressed solely in sentencing should he lose.

Later the Court further found those provisions of the federal Sentencing Reform Act of 1984 that make the guidelines mandatory also were unconstitutional.[18] So the Court "severed and excised" (in other words, removed) those provisions, making them, in essence, advisory only.[19] Instead of being bound by the sentencing guidelines, the Sentencing Reform Act, as revised by *Booker*, requires a sentencing court to consider guidelines ranges but permits the court to tailor the sentence in light of other statutory concerns as well. Thus, under *Booker*, sentencing courts must treat the guidelines as just one of a number of sentencing factors set forth in 18 U.S.C. Sec. 3553(a). The primary directive in section 3553(a) is for sentencing courts to "impose a sentence sufficient, but not greater than necessary, to comply with the purposes set forth in paragraph 2."

This being the case, if Alberto was convicted of this conspiracy, he would be looking at a mandatory minimum of thirty years based on the amount of drugs Amy said they had trafficked, even though there were no drugs actually observed, nor was there testimony about surveillance of actual large transactions. This was very hard to explain, and I often felt like an apologist for these terrible laws and the power of the prosecution in exercising discretion over what they charged, thus making it virtually impossible not to cooperate. I had to do it, though, because that was the reality.

"So how is this some big conspiracy? And how am I in it?" Alberto asked. Of course, Alberto wasn't saying he had nothing to do with drugs, but rather that there was no agreement, no enterprise, no gang. I ran through the facts with Alberto as I understood them based on my reading of the discovery. The central figure in this case was government witness Amy Pearson. Her testimony provided details of her drug distribution business and the conspiracy alleged in the indictment, involving distribution of multiple kilograms of cocaine between Chicago, Minnesota, and Florida. Amy and her family of coconspirators were targets of an investigation by the Minnesota Bureau of Criminal Apprehension. As part of the investigation, three family members' homes were wiretapped, with video cameras set up to monitor the outside of the homes. The investigation showed that the entire Pearson family was involved in narcotics trafficking, where Amy brought drugs from Chicago to distribute in Minnesota. After she and her family were arrested and charged in Minnesota with conspiracy to distribute narcotics, Amy agreed to cooperate in exchange for the government's recommendation of a sentence of seven and a half to thirteen and a half years. Alberto, if convicted, was a mandatory minimum of thirty years.

"I don't understand," he said. "If she the kingpin—wait, the queenpin"—he grinned as he said that—"how come she gets so little time?"

"Because we are a nation of snitches," I responded. "The only way to get under mandatory sentences or minimums is if the government gets cooperation, and then you become eligible for a much lower sentence."

Of course, I understand why the police and prosecution need to turn witnesses. Many prosecutions would not be possible without someone on the inside telling the story. The problem is that witnesses have motivation to try to read what the prosecution or police want and give it to them, to curry favor, and to lie to make their testimony seem more valuable. As I worked more on Alberto's case, I found that each of the "conspirators" slated to testify against him were women, white, or both. The only people being charged were Alberto and his friend Carlos Alvarez. It seemed to me that the prosecution was biased in terms of both race and gender.

"Well, can't we say something about that?" asked Alberto.

I sighed. I would have to tell him the story of John Bass, about how impossible it was to challenge racial bias in prosecution decision making. I had represented John in a federal death penalty prosecution in Detroit.[20] In his case, I raised the question of racial discrimination in the application of the federal death penalty in a pretrial motion to strike the notice of intent to seek the death penalty, and included a request for discovery from the federal government. When a claim of selective prosecution—or, in this context, selective selection for capital prosecution—is made, discovery is necessary to analyze whether or not the disparity noted can be explained by a race-neutral factor. The question is, what do you need to show in order to get the right to look at information that is normally not accessible to anyone outside the prosecutorial agency?

In this case, the motion to strike the death penalty notice was premised on the fact that in the years from January of 1995 through August of 1998 (the three years prior to the filing of the motion), 57 percent of the defendants for whom Attorney General Janet Reno had authorized the death penalty were Black.[21] African Americans were (and remain) vastly overrepresented among federal capital defendants, regardless of whether the baseline for comparison is the proportion of African Americans in the population of the United States (13 percent)[22] or the racial composition of defendants in federal prosecutions. African Americans represent 38 percent of the prisoners in federal prisons,[23] 33 percent of the defendants convicted in federal courts of violent offenses, 38 percent of the defendants convicted of drug offenses, and 27 percent of the offenders sentenced under the Federal Sentencing Guidelines.[24] Indeed, Professor Rory Little, a former member of the Capital Review Committee, states that "statistical race disparity persists in federal death penalty prosecutions. . . . [T]he bare statistics are disturbing. Far more black than white defendants are being submitted for DOJ capital case review and are being authorized for capital prosecution."[25]

In a civil context, statistics like these would undoubtedly create the prima facie case necessary to get discovery in a race discrimination case.[26] In the selective prosecution context, however, the burden is substantially higher—in fact, nearly impossibly high. In the older case of *Wayte v. United States*,[27] the Supreme Court held that "[i]t is appropriate to judge selective prosecution claims according to ordinary equal protection standards,"[28] and it was John's position that the same standard applied to his claim. However, the legal standard changed in 1996, so to succeed on his claim, John had to show that the federal prosecutorial policy had both a discriminatory *effect* and a discriminatory *intent* before he could even obtain discovery.[29]

If this standard is as high as the prosecution maintained, it would seem that defendants who were in a position to show both elements—discriminatory effect and intent—would need go no further; discovery would be unnecessary. If the standard was not that high—John need only show both discriminatory effect and the inference of discriminatory intent—then he should be able to get discovery.

The district court held that John had done enough to warrant discovery—the court's decision was informed by the national conversation at the time, including statistics and then–Attorney General Reno's expressions of concern at a press conference where she discussed the racial disparity their study revealed. Reno said that she was "troubled" by the study, and demanded an analysis of bias in the federal death penalty system. She called for studies by experts outside the department.[30] Then–Deputy Attorney General Eric Holder agreed with her concern, stating, "[N]o one reading this report can help but be disturbed, troubled by this disparity. We have to be honest with ourselves. Ours is still a race-conscious society, and yet people are afraid to talk about race."[31]

After the district court ordered the government to turn over discovery,[32] the government informed the court that it would not comply with that order, so the court dismissed the death penalty notice as a discovery sanction.[33] A divided panel of the United States Court of Appeals for the Sixth Circuit affirmed the district court's discovery order and remanded the case to the district court for further proceedings on issues of privilege, relevance, and undue burden that could not be addressed either by the district court or on appeal because the government had refused to produce any documents for the trial judge's consideration, *in camera* or otherwise.[34]

In a *per curiam* opinion, the United States Supreme Court granted certiorari and reversed.

In *United States v. Armstrong,* 517 U.S. 456, 465, 116 S.Ct. 1480, 134 L.Ed.2d 687 (1996), we held that a defendant who seeks discovery on a claim of selective prosecution must show some evidence of both discriminatory effect and discriminatory intent. We need go no further in the present case than consideration of the evidence supporting discriminatory effect. As to that, *Armstrong* says that the defendant must make a "credible showing" that "similarly situated individuals of a different race were not prosecuted." *Id.,* at 465, 470, 116 S.Ct. 1480. The Sixth Circuit concluded that respondent had made such a showing based on nationwide statistics demonstrating that "[t]he United States charges blacks with a death-eligible offense more than twice as often as it charges whites" and that the United States enters into plea bargains more frequently with whites than it does with blacks. 266 F. 3d 538–539. (citing U.S. Dept. of Justice, The Federal Death Penalty System: A Statistical Survey (1988–2000), p. 2 (Sept. 12, 2000). Even assuming that the *Armstrong* requirement can be satisfied by a nationwide showing (as opposed to a showing regarding the record of the decisionmakers in respondent's case), raw statistics regarding overall charges say nothing about charges brought against *similarly situated defendants.* And the statistics regarding plea bargains are even less relevant, since respondent *was* offered a plea bargain but

declined it. See Pet. for Cert. 16. Under *Armstrong*, therefore, because respondent failed to submit relevant evidence that similarly situated persons
were treated differently, he was not entitled to discovery.

The Sixth Circuit's decision is contrary to *Armstrong* and threatens the
"performance of a core executive constitutional function." *Armstrong,*
supra, at 465, 116 S.Ct. 1480. For that reason, we reverse.[35]

If there was any question after *Armstrong* about what it takes to get
discovery in order to mount a selective prosecution claim, *Bass* laid it
to rest. Without discovery, it is impossible to meet the burden necessary
to show there is no race-neutral way to explain the disparity and prevail.
In other words, you can't get there from here.

This is one of the reasons that a Defender General of the United
States is needed. Perhaps such an office could help the legislature and
the courts see that there has to be some way to get at racism within the
system.

I explained this to Alberto, and what was hard wasn't just how terrible the law was in this regard, but how unsurprised Alberto seemed.
It made me think about the seventh grade student's question at career
day, and the lack of surprise on the faces of those Black children when
I said the first thing I wanted to know about a new case was the color
of the victim.

"Look," he said, "I ain't a part of some conspiracy. Even if I wanted
to snitch, I don't know anything." He swallowed. "I got nothing to sell,"
he concluded.

How ironic, I thought. If he *were* a part of a drug conspiracy, he could
trade information for leniency, but because he was not, he had nothing
to trade and thus no way to lower his exposure.

"Do you want me to explore a plea offer?" I asked. "I could go to the
prosecutor and ask for the heaviest charges to be dropped in return for a
plea and some kind of agreement, or at least sentencing range, for you."

I could not be sure that any prosecutor would listen to me and just
give away the more serious charges. Sometimes when I try to explain
why I am not a very good negotiator, I tell people it is because the defense has only one power—the power to demand trial—and that power
can come with a very high price.

Alberto ran his hand through his hair and sighed. "Do we got a
chance at trial?" he asked.

"We have a chance," I replied, "but the odds are that the jury will convict you of *something*, given that there are seven counts, Even if the jury doesn't trust Pearson—the 'queenpin'"—I added that with a smile—"they will think you are involved somehow given that even though it was only a small amount, there was cocaine found at your place."

I paused and thought carefully before continuing on: "Look, as a lawyer, I would love to try your case. I think you are being offered as a sacrificial lamb, that the government is being unfair, and I think I can do damage to their case. What I worry about is the jury reacting to the stereotype of Latinos as drug dealers and that every voice will be lifted against you."

Alberto looked at me thoughtfully. "I can't let them get away with this," he said. "I would plead to the drugs they got me with—that's fair—but I can't do no more." He sat up straighter. "You good with that?"

I told him I was, and we went to trial. He was acquitted of five charges but convicted of one of the drug-dealing charges and possession. The judge reluctantly gave him the mandatory minimum of thirty years on the dealing charge. In 2015, he was granted clemency through the Clemency Project 2014, headed at that time by the esteemed Cynthia Roseberry; as of this writing, he is an over-the-road truck driver. The queenpin got out after only five years. About two years later, she wrote him a letter apologizing for lying.

If there were a Defender General, there would be an office to attack the way the system works, to support the work of the organizations that already are fighting the way the system works, and to support legislation that might decrease or eliminate the potential rewards for snitch evidence, which is often based on how "big" the cases are that are handed to the prosecution.

The United States needs a Defender General.

6

What a Defender General's Office Can Mean

In this book, we have been looking at the system. On many levels, it is clear that there needs to be some centralized and independent way to address the concerns raised here and to keep track of what we, as a country, are doing. While there are many well-intentioned legislative and other proposals out there, there is no one office that can even try to get at the center of the problem instead of just tinkering with "machinery of injustice," to paraphrase Justice Blackmun.[1]

The United States needs an office of the Defender General. To that end, I have been privileged to discuss this idea over many months with representatives of many organizations[2] as well as many individual attorneys, mitigation specialists, investigators, and the client community.[3] Our alliance has come up with a framework for the office:

The Defender General could advance Funding, Advocacy, and Policy.

I. Funding

By any measure—attorney pay, per capita funding, parity with prosecutors—public defense funding is insufficient. But the federal government need not wholly swap our paltry pecuniary patchwork with federal dollars to have an impact.

Vice President Kamala Harris's Fair and Just Defense Act (FJDA) would appropriate $250 million annually for public defense, conditioned on quality metrics and data collection. FJDA would both increase public defense investment and drive quality representation. The Office of the Defender General would be ideally suited to deploy FJDA funds and oversee progress:

- Incentivizing quality public defense through funding representation
- Creating quality metrics
- Collecting data

The Defender General's Funding Function could be modeled on the statewide public defense commissions in states like New York, Michigan, and Texas.

II. Advocacy
   Advocacy is central to advancing American public defense. The Defender General's Advocacy Function could not only weigh in on causes in the United States Supreme Court, it could also litigate Sixth Amendment violations by state and local actors:

- Represent defense interests in the United States Supreme Court
- Litigate Sixth Amendment violations by state and local actors
- Monitor compliance with consent decrees

The Defender General's Advocacy Function could be modeled in part on the Solicitor General and in part on the Civil Rights Division's enforcement mechanisms.

III. Policy
   Public defense has long suffered from a lack of clarity and focus. Unlike the prosecution function, the defense function has no central agency modeling best practices, informing lawmakers, or disseminating data. The Office of the Defender General could fulfill this role:

- Promoting standards
- Representing public defense at meetings and hearings
- Creating a clearinghouse for public defense data
- Supporting training, standards, and innovations
- Presentations and publications

The Defender General's Policy Function could be modeled in part on the Office of Justice Programs, including the Bureau of Justice Assistance, the Bureau of Justice Statistics, and the Office of Juvenile Justice and Delinquency Prevention.

Let me illustrate just how an office of the Defender General could address serious constitutional issues. After I left the Cook County Public Defender's office, I still had friends and colleagues there with whom I stayed in touch. As a professor, I could sometimes help someone there with a research project or brainstorming a case, and they often would do the same for me and my legal clinic, especially when I was at the DePaul University College of Law.

One former colleague was the redoubtable Mike Morrissey. He was the head of the felony trial division and one of the finest lawyers I have ever known. I once referred to him at an award ceremony as "the Jimmy Stewart of the public defender's office" and the sentiment was shared by many.

I got a call from him about a problem that Judge McHenry (not his real name) was giving the office about a potential death penalty case, one Mr. Maurice Dobson (not his real name either). Mr. Dobson was supposed to have been served with a search warrant, as a suspected high-level drug dealer, early one January morning. However, he was not in his home, as expected, but rather sitting in his parked car right outside the home. One of the arresting officers recognized him and began to approach. This is where things became chaotic. Someone started shooting, and pretty soon four different officers were shooting. Mr. Dobson was hit twelve times but survived. The police said he started the shooting, although no gun was found in the car and as far as could be determined, all the bullet holes seemed to have been from bullets coming in, not going out. During the melee a police officer was shot and killed. Because Mr. Dobson was alleged to have fired first, he was charged with that officer's murder under the felony murder doctrine.

The felony murder doctrine is meant to make all participants in a felony responsible for whatever happens during the course of a felony. So, for example, if you rob someone and they die of a heart attack during the robbery, that is felony murder. If you are the getaway driver and your compatriot shoots a bank guard and kills him as he runs from the bank robbery, and the prosecution is able to prove that beyond a reasonable doubt, you are guilty of felony murder. Similarly, if you and a compatriot try to rob a store and the store owner kills your friend, and that is proven beyond a reasonable doubt by the prosecution, you are guilty of felony murder. Thus if Mr. Dobson was guilty of aggravated battery by shooting his gun, the fact that "friendly fire" is what killed the police officer did not mean he couldn't be charged. In fact, he could be—and he was.

Mike told me all this when he called.

"Sounds like a tough case," I responded.

"Andrea, you are so right. But right now, we need to get him a lawyer."

"What?" I said. "I assumed that the public defender's office was his lawyer."

"Well, we were, but then McHenry decided that we couldn't be appointed unless Mr. Dobson filled out an affidavit of indigency." As a general rule, judges are supposed to determine whether a defendant is entitled to representation by the public defender by inquiring into his or her financial situation. In practice, anyone in custody charged with something this serious is pretty much automatically assigned to the office. Mike cleared his throat. "See, here is the problem. The police took everything out of his house, including a significant amount of cash. If he fills out this affidavit truthfully . . ."

I understood. If Mr. Dobson said he had no money, under oath, that could be perjury. If he acknowledged the money was his, that was awfully close to a confession at least to money laundering and likely drug dealing as well. Complicating matters even further, Mr. Dobson was still being treated for his many gunshot wounds and was on pain medications.

"How can I help?" I asked Mike.

"Well, we need to come up in some kind of way with a brief or something; it can't be right that to get his Sixth Amendment rights he has to give up his Fifth Amendment rights," Mike replied. In other words, in order to receive his constitutionally protected right to effective assistance—to a lawyer at all—as the Sixth Amendment requires, he would have to give up his constitutionally protected right to remain silent about potentially incriminating matters, under the Fifth Amendment. There was no win here.

I knew Mike was right and agreed to come in as a friend of the court, on a motion before both the presiding judge of the criminal division and Judge McHenry, saying just that. This was an issue that could affect many other defendants.

If, at the time of this arrest, there had been an Office of the Defender General, Mike could have called for help and perhaps suggested some policy-level meetings to resolve the issue. But there wasn't, so my students and I drafted the memorandum of law, filed it both places, and appeared in court on the day they were set in both places. After we finished filing our document with the presiding judge, he said he would take it under advisement and gave it a continuance date. I then went upstairs to Judge McHenry's courtroom to report this. When the case was called, I stepped up, identified myself as an amicus, and began to speak. I was interrupted.

"Are you filing an appearance on this case, Miss Lyon?" asked the judge. I should mention that I did not have a good history with Judge McHenry, having reversed him in another case, he thought unfairly.

"No, sir," I explained, "I am here as a friend of the court—" He interrupted me again.

"Then you have no right to speak." He raised his voice. "Mr. Sheriff, get her out of my courtroom." I was forcibly (but gently) removed. My students were horrified. I told them it had been at least twenty years since I had been thrown out of a courtroom and I appreciated the chance to feel young again. I didn't tell them how frightening and humiliating it was. But the truth was I didn't have standing unless the judge chose to give it to me, and the public defender's office couldn't speak either, because they had not been appointed.

Eventually, a lawyer from the public defender's office was appointed to Mr. Dobson, but it took months of time that could have been used to investigate and canvass for possible witnesses, visit the scene, view the evidence, and so much more.

If there were an Office of the Defender General, it could intervene or meet with the appropriate parties to explain why a defendant should not have to trade one constitutional right for another. But there wasn't, and there isn't. The United States needs a Defender General.

One critical reaction that I (and other members of the alliance) have heard about the idea of an Office of the Defender General is that it is too big an ask—that suggesting that we need to institutionalize and support our Constitution in this way is too big a criticism of how things have always been done, and that some institutions or people will react negatively to the idea because it is too big or too new.

To them I say, remember the one sure way to be certain that things do not change: Don't try. This book is intended to encourage all of those concerned about our country, our poor, and our broken criminal justice system to try. We should not be limited by what fixes have been proposed before or by what legislation has passed or failed to pass. We should strive for better, and we should ask for what is needed in the long run, not just small, immediate, news-driven reactions.

A major reason for making this effort is to hopefully succeed and for an Office of the Defender General to become a part of our government.

Another reason is that the conversations online, in the news, and in our homes, places of worship, at work, and among families, have been limited to reactions to individual cases or particular statutes—without addressing the need to have anything done systemically. They need not be, and even if it becomes discouraging to continue to fight, it is worth doing.

We should do this because it is the right thing to do for our country and our justice system, because it might just work, and, very importantly, because it may indeed lay the groundwork to get to systematic change in the future.

The need for criminal justice reform is salient and apparent. If, as a country, we are going to learn (or relearn) to trust our government and our justice system, we need to invest in measures that will build and sustain that trust—not just in response to headlines today, but in a sustained, thoughtful, and consistent way. This cannot happen if we continue to put Band-Aids on gaping wounds.

The United States needs a Defender General.

Notes

FOREWORD

As the deputy director for policy at the national ACLU, Roseberry works to transform federal, state, and local systems through legislative, administrative, electoral, and corporate advocacy. She focuses on the entire system, from policing, bail reform, trial, and sentencing to the death penalty and clemency.

During the Obama administration, she served as executive director of the historic Clemency Project 2014. Often referred to as the nation's largest law firm, with nearly four thousand lawyers, it provided pro bono support to obtain release for nearly two thousand people.

Roseberry was cited in Merriam-Webster's online dictionary when the word *decarceration* was entered.

Previously, Roseberry was the executive director of the Federal Defenders of the Middle District of Georgia, Inc. She has taught advanced criminal procedure and cotaught in the death penalty clinic at DePaul University College of Law in Chicago, where she also founded the misdemeanor clinic. For more than ten years prior to teaching, she practiced federal and state criminal defense in Georgia.

A founding board member of the Georgia Innocence Project, she was the first African American female president of the Georgia Association of Criminal Defense Lawyers. She received the 2016 COS Humanitarian Award, the 2017 annual service award from the Alpha Alpha Chapter of Phi Beta Sigma Fraternity, Incorporated, and the 2017 Champion of Justice Award from the National Association of Criminal Defense Lawyers.

1. BOB MARLEY AND THE WAILERS, *War*, on RASTAMAN VIBRATION (Island Records 1976).

2. Gideon v. Wainwright, 372 U.S. 335 (1963). See also In Re Gault, 387 U.S. 1 (1967), in which the right of a juvenile to have counsel was recognized.

3. Gideon v. Wainwright, 372 U.S. 335 (1963).

4. As a former public defender, I provide this description as a broad view of local, state, and federal systems. There are, without question, dedicated and competent indigent defense counsel across our nation.

INTRODUCTION

1. Not his real name. I am changing client, colleague, opponent, and judge names except where I have express permission to use their names. In pulling together the stories, thoughts, and ideas that comprise this book, I have called upon multiple prior works where I am the author. For a full list of these works, please visit www.andrealyon.com to view my curriculum vitae.

2. Faretta v. California, 422 U.S. 806 (1975).

3. Daniel Epps & William Ortman, *The Defender General*, 168 U. PA. L. REV. 1469 (2020). Notably, these authors recently proposed that a Defender General is needed to guide litigation specifically in the United States Supreme Court. They propose a federal-level office, and there are some parallels between their proposal and that of this book, although I propose a more policy-driven agenda that would influence not only Supreme Court litigation but defense, and specifically public defense, at all levels of the criminal justice system.

4. *Id.* at footnote 203. As part of their article and proposal, Epps and Ortman listed, to date, authors who referenced the idea of a Defender General:

See VT. STAT. ANN. tit. 13, § 5251 (2019) (creating the "Office of Defender General" to head public defense in Vermont); S. REP. No. 91-790, at 18 (1970) ("The [Senate Judiciary] committee recognizes the desirability of eventual creation of a strong, independent office to administer the Federal defender program. It considered as a possibility the immediate establishment of a new, independent official—a 'Defender General of the United States.'"); MODEL PUB. DEF. ACT § 10 (UNIF. LAW COMM'N 1970) (creating an Office of the Defender General, headed by an appointed "Defender General" who has "primary responsibility for providing needy persons with legal services"). A few scholars, moreover, have suggested that a federal "Defender General" could serve as a kind of political counterweight to the Attorney General. See Kenneth B. Nunn, The Trial as Text: Allegory, Myth and Symbol in the Adversarial Criminal Process—A Critique of the Role of the Public Defender and a Proposal for Reform, 32 AM. CRIM. L. REV. 743, 817 (1995) ("In order to balance the government's symbolic relationship to the criminal justice system, I would propose the creation of a 'Defender General' at the federal level. Like the Attorney General, the federal Defender General would also be a high government official, although not necessarily a member of the President's Cabinet."); Andrea D. Lyon, Dean's Desk: The United States Needs a Defender General, IND. LAW. (Oct. 18, 2016), https://www.theindianalawyer.com/articles/41749-deans-desk

-the-united-states-needs-a-defender-general [https://perma.cc/KBL9-7RMN] (arguing that a "defender general should command the same respect and stature that the offices of the attorney general and solicitor general command" and use its influence to "ensure that all of those interested in criminal justice have a seat at the table"). More recently, Matthew Segal of the ACLU of Massachusetts published an opinion piece in Slate arguing that a Defender General could counter a Department of Justice that is increasingly making "faulty," politically motivated arguments in court. Matthew R. Segal, The Census Case Shows Why We Need a Defender General, SLATE (June 27, 2019, 3:31 PM), https://slate.com/news-and-politics/2019/o6/doj-noel-francisco-lies-census-case-supremecourt-defender-general.html [https://perma.cc/9KBD-NBZW]. Segal's Defender General's Office, which would be more of a watchdog than a specialized Supreme Court advocate for criminal cases, would call the Department of Justice to task when it stepped out of line. See *Id.* Segal thus asks rhetorically whether DOJ brass would send "a career lawyer to quibble with federal judges about soap and blankets for detained kids if they had understood that a prestigious government-funded law office was prepared to tell the court that the DOJ's position was meritless?" *Id.* Segal's argument is premised on countering what we have called the Solicitor General's credibility advantage. See *supra* subsection I.B.3. Credibility is important, but like Senator Cory Booker's proposal (which Segal's op-ed notes), Segal's Defender General does not aim to solve the fundamental asymmetry in Supreme Court criminal litigation between the unified vision of prosecutors and the dispersed interests of defendants.

CHAPTER 1

1. Miranda v. Arizona, 384 U.S. 436 (1966).

2. Morgan v. Illinois, 504 U.S. 719 (1992).

3. See, e.g., Russell Stetler, *Mental Health Evidence and the Capital Defense Function: Prevailing Norms*, 82 UMKC L. REV. 407 (2014). See also Dorothy Roberts, *The Social and Moral Cost of Mass Incarceration in African American Communities.* 56 STAN. L. REV., 1271 (2003).

4. ANDREA D. LYON & MORT SMITH, TEAM DEFENSE IN CRIMINAL CASES (2014).

5. Laurence Steinberg & Elizabeth Scott, *Less Guilty by Reason of Adolescence: Developmental Immaturity, Diminished Responsibility, and the Juvenile Death Penalty*, 58 AM. PSYCH. 1009, 1014 (2003); Miller v. Alabama, 567 U.S. 460 (2012), Roper v. Simmons, 543 U.S. 551 (2005).

6. Atkins v. Virginia, 536 U.S. 304 (2002).

7. Historical research for this section was conducted by my colleague E. Kate Cohn as part of a research project regarding Sixth Amendment rights that she conducted for the National Association of Criminal Defense Lawyers.

8. U.S. Const. amend. VI.

9. Erica J. Hashimoto, *Resurrecting Autonomy: The Criminal Defendant's Right to Control the Case*, 90 B.U.L. REV. 1147, 1164 (2010).

10. *Id.*

11. *Id.* at 1165.

12. *Id.* at 1166.

13. Sanjay Chhablani, *Disentangling the Sixth Amendment*, 11 U. PA. J. CONST. L. 487, 492 (2009).

14. Hashimoto, at 1167.

15. *Id.* at 1168.

16. *Id.* at 1168.

17. Chhablani, at 492.

18. Powell v. Alabama, 287 U.S. 45, 53 (1932). Information about the right to choice of counsel, and its limitations, is summarized nicely here: https://law.jrank.org/pages/763/Counsel-Right-Counsel-right-counsel-one-s-choice.html#ixzz70nk4Urpz.

19. Wheat v. United States, 486 U.S. 153 (1988).

20. *Id.*; see also Johnson v. Zerbst, 304 U.S. 458, 58 S. Ct. 1019, 82 L. Ed. 1461 (1938).

21. Chhablani, at 494; see also Glasser v. United States, 315 U.S. 60, 62 S. Ct. 457, 86 L. Ed. 680 (1942).

22. Chhablani, at 494. For example, procedural protections extended to defendants in state courts and federal defendants were first granted the right to habeas corpus. The Chhablani article provides a nice historical overview of Sixth Amendment jurisprudence.

23. Gideon v. Wainwright, 372 U.S. 335, 344 (1963).

24. Hashimoto, at 1148; see also Gideon v. Wainwright, 372 U.S. 335, 344 (1963).

25. Hashimoto, at 1148.

26. Kimberly Helene Zelnick, *In Gideon's Shadow: The Loss of Defendant Autonomy and the Growing Scope of Attorney Discretion*, 30 AM. J. CRIM. L. 363, 373 (2003).

27. Strickland v. Washington, 466 U.S. 668 (1984).

28. *Id.* at 687.

29. *Id.* at 694.

30. McFarland v. State, 928 S.W.2d 482 (Tex. Crim. App. 1996) (per curiam), reh'g denied, 928 S.W.2d 482 (Tex. Crim. App. 1996), cert. denied sub nom. McFarland v. Texas, 519 U.S. 1119 (1997).

31. People v. Whitehead, 169 Ill 2d 355, 375 (1996).

32. Strickland v. Washington, 466 U.S. at 688.

33. *Id.*

34. Crisp v. Duckworth, 743 F.2d 580, 584 (7th Cir. 1984).

35. Morris v. Slappy, 461 U.S. 1 (1983).

36. *Id.*

37. United States v. Cronic, 466 U.S. at 657, n. 21.

38. *State Custody; Remedies in Federal Courts*, 28 U.S.C. § 2254.

39. Antiterrorism and Effective Death Penalty Act, 104, 110 Stat. at 1219.

40. *Id.*

41. *Id.*

42. Wainwright v. Sykes, 433 U.S. 72, 87 (1977).

43. *Id.*

44. Antiterrorism and Effective Death Penalty Act, 104, 110 Stat. at 1219.

45. Coleman v. Commonwealth, 226 Va. 31 (1983).

46. Coleman v. Thompson, 501 U.S. 722 (1991).

47. *See* Jennifer M. Allen, *Free for All a Free for All: The Supreme Court's Abdication of Duty in Failing to Establish Standards for Indigent Defense*, 27 LAW & INEQ. 365 (Summer 2009), in which the author explains that the courts have abdicated responsibility in this regard by being results oriented regarding the trial outcome rather than the constitutional right.

48. Lauren Sudeall Lucas, *Effectively Ineffective: The Failure of Courts to Address Underfunded Indigent Defense Systems*, HARV. L. REV., 118, 1731 (2004), in which the author argues that funding is unlikely to arise under the Strickland test for evaluating effective assistance of counsel because the test is oriented toward the ends rather than the means.

49. Better Government Association, *The High Cost of Wrongful Convictions*, BETTER GOVT ASSOC., http://www.bettergov.org/investigations/wrongful _convictions_1.aspx.

50. *Id.*

51. Connie McNeely, *Perceptions of the Criminal Justice System: Television Imagery and Public Knowledge in the United States*, 1 J. OF CRIM. JUST. AND POPULAR CULTURE, 3–5, 10 (1995).

52. David Harris, *The Appearance of Justice: Court TV, Conventional Television, and Public Understanding of the Criminal Justice System*, 35 ARIZ. L. REV. 785, 809 (1993).

53. Paul Colomy, *Making Youth Violence Visible: The News Media and the Summer of Violence*, 77 Denv. U. L. REV. 661, 672–73 (2000).

54. *Id.*; Aya Gruber, *Victim Wrongs: The Case for a General Criminal Defense Based on Wrongful Victim Behavior in an Era of Victims' Rights*, 76 TEMP. L. REV. 645 (2003).

55. Colomy, at 672–73.

56. DR. SUNWOLF, PRACTICAL JURY DYNAMICS: FROM ONE JUROR'S TRIAL PERCEPTIONS TO THE GROUPS'S DECISION-MAKING PROCESS (2004); Richard K. Gabriel, *Values, Beliefs, and Demographics in Selecting Jurors*, ATLA-CLE 49 (Winter 2002).

57. Sunwolf, *supra* note 56; Gabriel, *supra* note 56.

58. Harris, at 786.

59. Ray Surette, *The Media, the Public and Criminal Justice Policy,* 2 J. INST. JUST. INT'L STUD. 39, 43 (2003).

60. Sara Sun Beale, *The News Media's Influence on Criminal Justice Policy: How Market-driven News Promotes Punitiveness,* 48 WM. & MARY L. REV. 397, 459 (2006).

61. Sarah Eschholz, *Crime on Television: Issues in Criminal Justice,* 9 J. INST. JUST. INT'L STUD. 9, 9–11 (2003).

62. California v. Hodari D., 499 U.S. 621, 623 n.1 (1991), where Justice Antonin Scalia criticized the state's concession that it would be unreasonable to stop, for brief inquiry, young men who scatter in panic upon the mere sighting of the police as it is not self-evident, and arguably contradicts proverbial common sense. See Proverbs 28:1 ("The wicked flee when no man pursueth"); Mia Carpiniello, *Striking a Sincere Balance: A Reasonable Black Person Standard For "Location Plus Evasion" Terry Stops,* 6 MICH. J. RACE & L. 355, 357–70 (2001); Cynthia Kwei Yung Lee, *Race and Self-Defense: Towards a Normative Conception of Reasonableness,* 81 MINN. L. REV. 367, 455–70 (1996).

63. WANDA M. L. LEE, CROSS CULTURING COUNSELING, 75–76 (1999).

64. U.S. v. Wade, 388 U.S. 218, 228 (1967); Benjamin Rosenberg, *Rethinking the Right to Due Process in Connection with Pre-trial Identification Procedures: an Analysis and a Proposal,* 79 KY. L.J. 259, 260 (1990/1991).

65. Kimberlianne Podlas, *As Seen on TV: The Normative Influence of Syndicourt on Contemporary Litigiousness,* 11 VILL. SPORTS & ENT. L.J. 1, 19–23 (2004).

CHAPTER 2

1. Miranda v. Arizona, 384 U.S. 436 (1966).

2. *Central Park Five: The True Story behind When They See Us,* BBC NEWS, June 12, 2019, https://www.bbc.com/news/newsbeat-48609693.

3. California Innocence Project, *False Testimony/Confessions,* https://cali forniainnocenceproject.org/issues-we-face/false-confessions/#:~:text=One%20 of%20the%20most%20well,pressure%20to%20find%20those%20responsible.

4. Samson J. Schatz, *Interrogated with Intellectual Disabilities: The Risks of False Confession,* 70 STAN. L. REV. 643, 651 (2018).

5. National Registry of Exonerations, *False Confessions,* https://www.law .umich.edu/special/exoneration/Pages/False-Confessions.aspx.

6. Connick v. Thompson, 563 U.S. 51 (2011).

7. Michael Wines, *Prosecutors Had the Wrong Man. They Prosecuted Him Anyway*, N. Y. TIMES, Jan. 17, 2018, https://www.nytimes.com/2018/01/17/us/prosecutors-new-orleans-evidence.html.

8. Connick v. Thompson, 563 U.S. 51 (2011).

9. *Id.*

10. The discussion of the education and training (and lack thereof) regarding prosecutorial conduct is supported by my colleague's research. *See* Kate Cohn, *When the Home Team Calls Their Own Balls and Strikes: The Problem of Brady Violations, Accountability, and Making the Case for a Washington State Commission on Prosecutorial Conduct*, 19 SEATTLE J. FOR SOC. JUST. 161 (2020).

11. Robert Granfield & Thomas Koenig, *It's Hard to Be a Human Being and a Lawyer: Young Attorneys and the Confrontation with Ethical Ambiguity in Legal Practice*, 105 W. L. REV. 495, 502 (2003). The authors offer examples of professional development organizations using ethics guidelines as a mechanism not for enforcement, but as a smoke screen to offer appearances of accountability in what can be deemed self-monitored professions. Statistics derived from the ABA validate this assertion as far as Washington State is concerned.

12. *Id.* at 500.

13. *Id.*

14. *Id.*

15. ABA, STANDING COMM. ON PRO. REGUL. OF THE AM. BAR ASS'N CTR. FOR PRO. RESP., 2017 SURVEY ON LAWYER DISCIPLINE SYSTEMS (2019), http://www.americanbar.org/content/dam/aba/administrative/professional_responsibility/2017sold-results.pdf [https://perma.cc/ER4Q-VDEM].

16. *Id.* at chart I pt. A, chart III pt.A, chart III pt.B.

17. See *id.* at chart IX pt.A.

18. *Id.*

19. Debra Cassens Weiss, *Sleeping Lead Lawyer Doesn't Justify Overturning Capital Conviction, Federal Judge Rules*, ABA J., April 10, 2019, https://www.abajournal.com/news/article/sleeping-lead-lawyer-doesnt-justify-over turning-capital-conviction-federal-judge-rules. Ultimately, the case received such widespread publicity that his death sentence was overturned, and he pled guilty for a term of imprisonment. See Henry Weinstein, *Inmate in Texas Sleeping-Lawyer Case Pleads Guilty*, L.A. TIMES, June 20, 2003, https://www.latimes.com/archives/la-xpm-2003-jun-20-na-sleep20-story.html.

20. Debra Cassens Weiss, *Contract Public Defenders in this State Make About $5 per Hour after Overhead, New Study Says*, ABA J., July 9, 2020, https://www.abajournal.com/news/article/contract-public-defenders-in-this-state-make-about-5-an-hour-after-overhead-study-says.

21. Adam Walinsky, *What It's Like to Be in Hell*, N. Y. TIMES, Dec. 4, 1987, https://www.nytimes.com/1987/12/04/opinion/what-it-s-like-to-be-in -hell.html

22. The Bail Project, *After Cash Bail: A Framework for Reimagining Pretrial Justice*, https://bailproject.org/after-cash-bail/.

23. Joseph Goldstein, *Teenager Claims Body-Cams Show the Police Framed Him. What Do You See?* N. Y. TIMES, Nov. 19, 2018, https://www.ny times.com/2018/11/19/nyregion/body-cameras-police-marijuana-arrest.html.

24. ELIZABETH LOFTUS & KATHERINE KETCHAM, WITNESS FOR THE DEFENSE: THE ACCUSED, THE EYEWITNESS, AND THE EXPERT WHO PUTS MEMORY ON TRIAL (1991); JIM DWYER, PETER J. NEUFELD, & BARRY SCHECK, ACTUAL INNOCENCE: FIVE DAYS TO EXECUTION AND OTHER DISPATCHES FROM THE WRONGLY CONVICTED (2000); JENNIFER THOMPSON-CANNINO, RONALD COTTON, & ERIN TORNEO, PICKING COTTON: OUR MEMOIR OF INJUSTICE AND REDEMPTION (2009).

25. BRANDON GARRETT, CONVICTING THE INNOCENT (2011).

26. National Registry of Exonerations, *Exonerations by Year, DNA and Non-DNA*, https://www.law.umich.edu/special/exoneration/Pages/Exoneration -by-Year.aspx.

27. Innocence Project, www.innocenceproject.org. It is important to realize that DNA is not available in the majority of criminal cases. As such, these DNA exoneration cases likely represent just the tip of the iceberg.

28. Much of this section comes from discussion with, and an expert report by, Dr. Berkowitz in the post-conviction case of People v. Dreshawn Luna, No. 10-CF-4004, which is pending in the trial court of Lake County, Illinois, at the time of this writing.

29. Richard A. Leo & Brittany Liu, *What Do Potential Jurors Know About Police Interrogation Techniques and False Confessions*, 27 BEHAV. SCI. & L. 381 (2009).

30. Tanja Rapus Benton et al., *Eyewitness Memory Is Still Not Common Sense: Comparing Jurors, Judges and Law Enforcement to Eyewitness Experts*, 20.1 APP. COG. PSYCH.: THE OFF. J. OF THE SOC. FOR APP. RES. IN MEM. AND COG. 115–29 (2006); Kenneth A. Deffenbacher & Elizabeth F. Loftus, *Do Jurors Share a Common Understanding Concerning Eyewitness Behavior?* 6.1 LAW AND HUM. BEHAV. 15–30 (1982); R. S. Schmechel et al., *Beyond the Ken? Testing Jurors' Understanding of Eyewitness Reliability Evidence*, 46 JURIMETRICS 177 (2006); Daniel J. Simons & Christopher F. Chabris, *What People Believe about How Memory Works: A Representative Survey of the US Population*, 6.8 PLOS ONE (2011); Richard Wise et al., *What US Prosecutors and Defence Attorneys Know and Believe about Eyewitness Testimony*, 23.9 APP. COG. PSYCH.: THE OFF. J. OF THE SOC. FOR APP. RES. IN MEM. AND COG, 1266–1281 (2009); Richard A Wise, Martin A. Safer, & Christina M. Maro, *What US Law Enforce-*

ment Officers Know and Believe about Eyewitness Factors, Eyewitness Interviews and Identification Procedures, 25.3 App. Cog. Psych. 488–500 (2011).

31. Manson v. Brathwaite, 432 U.S. at 114.

32. Timothy P. O'Toole & Giovanna Shay, *Manson v. Brathwaite Revisited: Towards a New Rule of Decision for Due Process Challenges to Eyewitness Identification Procedures*, 41 Val. U.L. Rev. 112–13 (Fall 2006).

33. *Id.* at 113.

34. Deputy Attorney General Sally Q. Yates, *Eyewitness Identification: Procedures for Conducting Photo Arrays: Memorandum for Heads of Department Law Enforcement Components All Department Prosecutors* (Jan. 6, 2017), https://www.justice.gov/file/923201/download.

35. FindLaw, *What Is Prosecutorial Discretion?* https://www.findlaw.com /criminal/criminal-procedure/what-is-prosecutorial-discretion-.html #:~:text=Prosecutorial%20discretion%20is%20when%20a,which%20criminal%20charges%20to%20file.

36. Megan T. Stevenson, *Distortion of Justice: How the Inability to Pay Bail Affects Case Outcomes*, 34 J. of L., Econ., & Org 511–42 (2018).

37. William Ortman, *Second-Best Criminal Justice*, 96 Wash. U.L. Rev. 1061, 1066 (2019).

38. *Id.*

39. *Id.*

40. *Id.* at 1070.

41. Sentencing Project, *State by State Data*, https://www.sentencingproject. org/the-facts/#map?dataset-option=SIR. This interactive website allows users to see incarceration rates by state and also view racial disparities and juvenile sentencing statistics.

42. Missouri v. Frye, 566 U.S. 133, 144 (2012), quoting Robert E. Scott & William J. Stuntz, *Plea Bargaining as Contract*, 101 Yale L.J. 1909, 1912 (1992).

43. Rick Jones, Gerald B. Lefcourt, Barry J. Pollack, Norman L. Reimer, & Kyle O'Dowd, *The Trial Penalty: The Sixth Amendment Right to Trial on the Verge of Extinction and How to Save It*, National Association of Criminal Defense Lawyers, 4–5, 2018, https://www.nacdl.org/getattachment/95b7f0f5 -90df-4f9f-9115-520b3f58036a/the-trial-penalty-the-sixth-amendment-right -to-trial-on-the-verge-of-extinction-and-how-to-save-it.pdf.

44. Anna Offit, *Prosecuting in the Shadow of the Jury*, 113 NW. U. L. Rev. 1071, 1083 (2019).

45. Rick Jones et al., at 9.

46. *Id.*

47. *Id.*

48. *Id.* at 4–5.

49. Ortman, at 1083.

CHAPTER 3

1. McCleskey v. Kemp, 481 U.S. 279 (1987).

2. See, e.g., MICHELLE ALEXANDER, THE NEW JIM CROW: MASS INCARCERATION IN THE AGE OF COLORBLINDNESS (2010); BRYAN STEVENSON, JUST MERCY: A STORY OF JUSTICE AND REDEMPTION (2014).

3. Katesha Long, *Debunking the Broken Windows Theory in Policing: An Incident and Badge of Slavery*, 4 How. HUM. & CIV. RTS. L. REV. 77 (2020).

4. Curtis Bunn, *10 Slave Codes That Were Designed to Oppress and Humiliate Black People*, ATLANTA BLACK STAR (Dec. 22, 2014), https://atlantablackstar.com/2014/12/22/10-slave-codes-that-were-designed-to-oppress-and-humiliate-black-people/.

5. Alan K. Lamm, *Slave Codes*, NCPEDIA (2006), https://www.ncpedia.org/slave-codes.

6. U.S. Const. amend. XIII, § 1.

7. History.com Editors, *Black Codes*, HISTORY, https://www.history.com/topics/black-history/black-codes.

8. Roberto Tijerina, *Black Codes, Jim Crow, and Social Control in the South*, STMU HISTORY MEDIA (Mar. 22, 2017), https://www.stmuhistorymedia.org/the-south-and-vigilante-justice/.

9. History.com Editors, *Black Codes*.

10. Nadra Kareem Nittle, *The Black Codes and Why They Still Matter Today*, THOUGHT Co., https://www.thoughtco.com/the-black-codes-4125744.

11. Long, at 77.

12. The Civil Rights Bill of 1866, HISTORY, ART, & ARCHIVES UNITED STATES HOUSE OF REPRESENTATIVES, https://history.house.gov/Historical-Highlights/1851-1900/The-Civil-Rights-Bill-of-1866/.

13. Drug Policy Alliance, *Race and the Drug War,* https://drugpolicy.org/issues/race-and-drug-war.

14. *Id.*

15. *Id.*

16. Ernest F. Lidge III, *Perp Walks and Prosecutioral Ethics,* 7 NEV. L. J. 55 (2006–2007). See also Scott Sayare et al., *French Shocked by I.M.F. Chief's 'Perp Walk,'* N. Y. TIMES, http://thelede.blogs.nytimes.com/2011/05/16/french-shocked-by-i-m-f-chiefs-perp-walk/.

17. ABA MODEL RULES OF PROF'L CONDUCT R. 3.8(f). (2013).

18. Lidge, at 60, citing Caldarola v. Co. of Westchester, 343 F.3d 570 (2d Cir. 2003).

19. *Id.*

20. The discussion of the historical roots relies heavily on my colleague's research. See Kate Cohn, *When the Home Team Calls Their Own Balls and Strikes: The Problem of Brady Violations, Accountability, and Making the Case*

for a Washington State Commission on Prosecutorial Conduct, 19 SEATTLE J. FOR SOC. JUST 161 (2020).

21. Thomas P. Sullivan & Maurice Possley, *The Chronic Failure to Discipline Prosecutors for Misconduct: Proposals for Reform*, 105 J. CRIM. L. & CRIMINOLOGY 881, 923 (2015).

22. Imbler v. Pachtman, 424 U.S. 409, 422–23 (1976).

23. At time of original statute, it read, in part:

An Act to enforce the Provisions of the Fourteenth Amendment to the Constitution of the United States, and for other Purposes.

Be it enacted . . . That any person who, under color of any law, statute, ordinance, regulation, custom, or usage of any State, shall subject, or cause to be subjected any person within the jurisdiction of the United States to the deprivation of any rights, privileges, or immunities secured by the Constitution of the United States, shall, any such law, statute, ordinance, regulation, custom or usage of the State to the contrary notwithstanding, be liable to the party injured in any action at law, suit in equity, or other proper proceeding for redress; such proceeding to be prosecuted in the several district or circuit courts of the United States, with and subject to the same rights of appeal, review upon error, and other remedies provided in like cases in such courts, under the provisions of the [Civil Rights Act of 1866], and the other remedial laws of the United States which are in their nature applicable in such cases.

Ku Klux Klan Act of 1871, ch. 22, 17 Stat. 13 (1871) (codified at 42 U.S.C. § 1983), https://www.law.cornell.edu/uscode/text/42/1983.

24. *Id.*

25. Margaret Z. Johns, *Unsupportable and Unjustified: A Critique of Absolute Prosecutorial Immunity*, 80 FORDHAM L. REV. 509, 510 (2011).

26. *Id.* at 526.

27. David Keenan et al., *Myth of Prosecutorial Accountability after* Connick v. Thompson*: Why Existing Professional Responsibility Measures Cannot Protect Against Prosecutorial Misconduct*, 121 YALE L.J. F. 203, 214 (2012).

28. Johns, at 526.

29. Griffith v. Slinkard, 44 N.E. 1001, 1002 (1896).

30. *Id.* See also Johns, at 526.

31. Griffith, 44 N.E. at 1001.

32. *Id.*

33. *Id.*, quoting JOHN TOWNSHEND, A TREATISE ON THE WRONGS CALLED SLANDER & LIBEL (3d Ed.), § 227, pp. 395–96.

34. Imbler v. Pachtman, 424 U.S. 409, 422 (1976).

35. *Id.*

36. *Id.* at 415.

37. *Id.*

38. *Id.*

39. *Id.* at 431.

40. *Id.* at 428, quoting Gregoire v. Biddle, 177 F.2d 579, 581 (2d Cir. 1949).

41. *Id.*

42. *Id.* at 424.

43. *Id.*

44. Johns, at 526–27.

45. *Id.* at 510.

46. *Id.* at 526.

47. *Id.* at 526–27.

48. *Id.*

49. See ANDREA D. LYON, ANGEL OF DEATH ROW: MY LIFE AS A DEATH PEN-ALTY DEFENSE LAWYER, chs. 4 & 5 (2010).

50. Illinois no longer has a death penalty, so while my former unit still handles homicide cases, it does not handle people facing the death penalty anymore. Christopher Wills, *Illinois Death Penalty Abolished: Pat Quinn Signs Death Penalty Ban, Clears Death Row*, HUFFINGTON POST, Mar. 9, 2011, http://www.huffingtonpost.com/2011/03/08/illinois-death-penalty-ab_n_833250.html.

51. See ROGER PRZYBYLSKI ET AL., TRENDS AND ISSUES, 1997: ILLINOIS CRIMI-NAL JUSTICE INFORMATION AUTHORITY 77 (1997).

52. Public Act 099-0258; 705 ILCS 405/5-130.

53. United States ex rel. Griffith v. Hulick, 587 F. Supp. 2d 899, 902 (N.D. Ill. 2008).

54. *Id.*

55. Edmonson v. Leesville Concrete Co., 500 U.S. 614, 633–34 (1991).

56. See, e.g., Rachel V. Lyon (Director), *Juror Number 6*, DVD. https://www.amazon.com/Juror-Number-Six-Educational-Performance/dp/1463105207/ref=sr_1_1?keywords=Juror+Number+6&qid=1648836846&sr=8-1.

57. People v. Lerma, 2016 IL 118496, ¶¶ 24–25, 47 N.E.3d 985.

58. *Id.*

59. *Id. See also* Commonwealth v. Walker, 625 Pa. 450, 92 A.3d 766, 782–83 (Pa. 2014); State v. Guilbert, 306 Conn. 218, 49 A.3d 705, 723–24 (Conn. 2012); State v. Dubose, 2005 WI 126, 285 Wis. 2d 143, 699 N.W.2d 582, 591–92 (Wis. 2005).

60. Walker, 625 Pa. at 476–78.

61. The discussion of eyewitness identification and research extracted from affidavit of Dr. Shari R. Berkowitz, prepared for People v. Luna (No. 10-CF-4004).

62. ELIZABETH F. LOFTUS, EYEWITNESS TESTIMONY (1979).

63. Elizabeth Loftus, *How Reliable Is Your Memory*, TED, (2013), http://www.ted.com/talks/elizabeth_loftus_the_fiction_of_memory.html. TED is a

global non-profit organization that spreads ideas through "short, powerful" talks. Created in 1984, by 2012, TED Talks (which are published online) received over 1 billion views.

64. Linda J. Levine & David A. Pizarro, *Emotion and Memory Research: A Grumpy Overview*, 22 SOCIAL COGNITION, 530–54 (2005).

65. Jennifer M. Talarico & David C. Rubin, *Confidence, Not Consistency, Characterizes Flashbulb Memories*, 14 PSYCH. SCI, 455–61 (2003).

66. Cara Laney & Elizabeth Loftus, *Emotional Content of True and False Memories*, 16 MEMORY, 500–16 (2008).

67. ELIZABETH LOFTUS & KATHERINE KETCHAM, WITNESS FOR THE DEFENSE: THE ACCUSED, THE EYEWITNESS, AND THE EXPERT WHO PUTS MEMORY ON TRIAL (1991); JIM DWYER, PETER J. NEUFELD, & BARRY SCHECK, ACTUAL INNOCENCE: FIVE DAYS TO EXECUTION AND OTHER DISPATCHES FROM THE WRONGLY CONVICTED (2000); JENNIFER THOMPSON-CANNINO, RONALD COTTON, & ERIN TORNEO, PICKING COTTON: OUR MEMOIR OF INJUSTICE AND REDEMPTION (2009).

68. Dwyer et al., (2000).

69. Laura Connelly, *Cross-Racial Identifications: Solutions to the They All Look Alike Effect*, 21 MICH. J. RACE & L. 125 (2015), https://repository.law.umich.edu/cgi/viewcontent.cgi?article=1052&context=mjrl.

70. Tanja Rapus Benton et al., *Eyewitness Memory Is Still Not Common Sense: Comparing Jurors, Judges and Law Enforcement to Eyewitness Experts*, 20.1 APP. COG. PSYCH.: THE OFF. J. OF THE SOC. FOR APP. RES. IN MEM. AND COG. 115–29 (2006); Kenneth A. Deffenbacher & Elizabeth F. Loftus, *Do Jurors Share a Common Understanding Concerning Eyewitness Behavior?* 6.1 LAW AND HUM. BEHAV. 15–30 (1982); R. S. Schmechel et al., *Beyond the Ken? Testing Jurors' Understanding of Eyewitness Reliability Evidence*, 46 JURIMETRICS 177 (2006); Daniel J. Simons & Christopher F. Chabris, *What People Believe about How Memory Works: A Representative Survey of the US Population*, 6.8 PLoS ONE (2011); Richard Wise et al., *What US Prosecutors and Defence Attorneys Know and Believe about Eyewitness Testimony*, 23.9 APP. COG. PSYCH.: THE OFF. J. OF THE SOC. FOR APP. RES. IN MEM. AND COG, 1266–81 (2009); Richard A Wise, Martin A. Safer, & Christina M. Maro, *What US Law Enforcement Officers Know and Believe about Eyewitness Factors, Eyewitness Interviews and Identification Procedures*, 25.3 APP. COG. PSYCH. 488–500 (2011).

71. L. Song Richardson, *Arrest Efficiency and the Fourth Amendment*, 95 MINN. L. REV. 2035, 2044 (2011).

72. See Jeffrey J. Rachlinski et al., *Does Unconscious Racial Bias Affect Trial Judges?* 84 NOTRE L. REV. 1195, 1196 (2009).

73. Catherine Smith, *Unconscious Bias and "Outsider" Interest Convergence*, 40 CONN. L. REV. 1077, 1086 (2008), quoting Catherine E. Smith, *The Group Dangers of Race-Based Conspiracies*, 59 RUTGERS L. REV. 55, 82–83 (2006).

74. Batson v. Kentucky, 476 U.S. 79, 82 (1986).

75. People v. Randall, 283 Ill. App. 3d 1019, 1026, 671 N.E.2d 60, 66 (1st Dist. 1996).

76. AP, *Cops Bought Burger King for Dylann Roof Following His Arrest*, ABC News, June 23, 2015, https://abc7.com/dylann-roof-south-carolina-church-shooting-emanuel-african-methodist-episcopal/801013/. While much can be said about an arrestee's right to humane treatment, there are many documented stories of Black and brown arrestees treated inhumanely, even tortured, rather than provided a hamburger because "he hadn't eaten, they said, in a couple of days."

CHAPTER 4

1. Jonathan Rapping, Gideon's Promise: A Public Defender Movement to Transform Criminal Justice 53–153 (Beacon Press 2020).

2. Juliet Sorenson, *Ten Years Ago Illinois Abolished the Death Penalty. These People Helped Make It Happen*, Injustice Watch, May 7, 2021, https://www.injusticewatch.org/commentary/2021/illinois-death-penalty-abolition/.

3. The moment of abolition, effected by then-governor Pat Quinn with a stroke of the pen, capped years of advocacy by a wide range of stakeholders. They included individuals who had been wrongfully convicted and sentenced to death, faith-based leaders, journalists, community organizers, families of victims of crime, and elected officials.

4. Alafair S. Burke, *Prosecutorial Agnosticism*, 8 Ohio St. J. Crim. L. 79 (2010).

5. Emily Yoffe, *Innocence Is Irrelevant*, The Atlantic, September 2017, https://www.theatlantic.com/magazine/archive/2017/09/innocence-is-irrelevant/534171/.

6. Eyal Press, *A Fight to Expose the Hidden Human Costs of Incarceration*, The New Yorker, Aug 16, 2021, https://www.newyorker.com/magazine/2021/08/23/a-fight-to-expose-the-hidden-human-costs-of-incarceration.

Andrea Armstrong worked to understand how death was impacted individuals incarcerated in her home state of Louisiana. She ended up creating an interactive database, https://www.incarcerationtransparency.org/, that allows users to view prison deaths parish by parish. This work, along with the work of the various other organizations referenced throughout (Marshall Project, Innocence Project, Vera Institute, etc.) should have representation through the Defender General.

7. United States Dept. of Justice, *Justice Manual, Title 9, Criminal, Capital Crimes*, https://www.justice.gov/jm/jm-9-10000-capital-crimes.

8. This section, exploring *Brady* violations, borrows heavily from my colleague Kate Cohn's research on the issue. See Kate Cohn, *When the Home Team Calls Their Own Balls and Strikes: The Problem of Brady Violations, Accountability, and Making the Case for a Washington State Commission on Prosecutorial Conduct*, 19 SEATTLE J. FOR SOC. JUST 161 (2020).

9. Margaret Z. Johns, *Unsupportable and Unjustified: A Critique of Absolute Prosecutorial Immunity*, 80 FORDHAM L. REV. 509, 526–27 (2011).

10. David Keenan et al., *Myth of Prosecutorial Accountability after* Connick v. Thompson: *Why Existing Professional Responsibility Measures Cannot Protect against Prosecutorial Misconduct*, 121 YALE L.J. F. 203, 204 (2012).

11. Jason Kreag, *Disclosing Prosecutorial Misconduct*, 72 VAND. L. REV. 297, 305–306 (2019).

12. Brady v. Maryland, 373 U.S. 83, 87 (1963).

13. *Id.*

14. *Id.* at 87–88. Within this eloquent part of the opinion, the *Brady* court quoted Frederick William Lehmann, who was appointed solicitor general by President William Howard Taft in 1910. *See also* Jeremy L. Carlson, *The Professional Duty of Prosecutors to Disclose Exculpatory Evidence to the Defense: Implications of Rule 3.8(D) of the Model Rules of Professional Conduct*, 28 J. LEGAL PRO. 125, 126 (2004); U.S. DEP'T OF JUST., OFF. OF SOLIC. GEN., SOLIC. GEN. FREDERICK WILLIAM LEHMANN (2019), https://www.justice.gov/osg/bio /frederick-w-lehmann [https://perma.cc/KHC2-6VH9].

15. Thomas P. Sullivan & Maurice Possley, *The Chronic Failure to Discipline Prosecutors for Misconduct: Proposals for Reform*, 105 J. CRIM. L. & CRIMINOLOGY 881, 914 (2015). See also United States v. Agurs, 427 U.S. 97 (1976); United States v. Bagley, 473 U.S. 667 (1985); Kyles v. Whitley, 514 U.S. 419 (1995).

While most practitioners in, and scholars of, the legal profession are well versed in the term "*Brady* violation," the scope of obligations laid out in *Brady* has been distinctly nuanced by at least three additional United States Supreme Court cases: *United States v. Agurs, United States v. Bagley*, and *Kyles v. Whitley*. Each of these cases articulates how *Brady* places decision making about the rules in the hands of prosecutors—the very cadre of attorneys for whom the rules were created. From 1963 to 1995, an evolution occurred from *Brady*, where the Court required that a defendant make a request for evidence, to *Kyles*, where the Court placed responsibility on the prosecution to disclose known, favorable evidence. In *Agurs* and *Bagley*, the Court set standards for perjured evidence and materiality. While these subsequent cases helped clarify prosecutors' *Brady* obligations, many prosecutors still knowingly and unknowingly conduct themselves in ways that violate *Brady*.

16. Sullivan & Possley, at 914.

17. *Id.*

18. *Id.* at 915 n.131.

19. *Id.*

20. *Id.*

21. See Brady v. Maryland, 373 U.S. 83, 87 (1963).

22. See Agurs, 427 U.S. 97; Bagley, 473 U.S. 667; Kyles, 514 U.S. 419. See also Keenan et al., at 207.

23. Sullivan & Possley, at 914.

24. Lara A. Bazelon, *Hard Lessons: The Role of Law Schools in Addressing Prosecutorial Misconduct*, 16 BERKELEY J. CRIM. L. 391, 411 (2011).

25. *Id.*

26. *Id.* at 515.

27. Sullivan & Possley, at 884 n.5.

28. Johns, at 516.

29. *Id.* at 515.

30. Sullivan & Possley, at 884.

31. *Id.*

32. Johns, at 516.

33. *Id.*

34. NAT'L ARCHIVES, FED. REG., ANN. DETERMINATION OF AVERAGE COST OF INCARCERATION FEE (COIF) (2019), https://www.federalregister.gov/documents/2019/11/19/2019-24942/annual-determination-of-average-cost-of-incarceration-fee-coif [https://perma.cc/RS3J-V883].

35. *Id.* For example, in Washington State, the cost for incarceration in fiscal year 2018, per inmate, ranged from $32,000 to $40,000, depending on the facility.

36. Johns, 515–16.

37. Adam M. Gershowitz, *Prosecutorial Shaming: Naming Attorneys to Reduce Prosecutorial Misconduct*, 42 U.C. DAVIS L. REV. 1059, 1075 (2008).

38. *Id.*

39. *Id.* at 1066.

40. *Id.* at 1068. In discussing a specific case to illustrate this problem, the author notes:

> Despite . . . egregious misconduct, the Court never identified the prosecutors involved. Instead, in the introduction and factual history section of its opinion, the Court referred forty-two times to "the State" and "the prosecutors." In many of these instances and other references throughout the body of the opinion, it would have made more sense grammatically to use the prosecutors' actual names.

41. *Id.* at 1071–74.

42. *Id.* at 1074.

43. *Id.*

44. *Id.*

45. *Id.*

46. *Id.*

47. *Id.*

48. Connick v. Thompson, 563 U.S. 51, 60 (2011).

49. SAMUEL R. GROSS, MAURICE J. POSSLEY, KAITLIN JACKSON ROLL, & KLARA HUBER STEPHENS, GOVERNMENT MISCONDUCT AND CONVICTING THE INNOCENT: THE ROLE OF PROSECUTORS, POLICE AND OTHER LAW ENFORCEMENT 76 (2020), https://www.law.umich.edu/special/exoneration/Documents/Government_Miscon duct_and_Convicting_the_Innocent.pdf [https://perma.cc/Q333-3GWY] at 102.

50. Johns, *at* 520. The code, titled Deprivation of Rights Under Color of Law (18 U.S.C. § 242 [1996]), reads:

> Whoever, under color of any law, statute, ordinance, regulation, or custom, will-fully subjects any person in any State, Territory, Commonwealth, Possession, or District to the deprivation of any rights, privileges, or immunities secured or pro-tected by the Constitution or laws of the United States, or to different punishments, pains, or penalties, on account of such person being an alien, or by reason of his color, or race, than are prescribed for the punishment of citizens, shall be fined under this title or imprisoned not more than one year, or both; and if bodily injury results from the acts committed in violation of this section or if such acts include the use, attempted use, or threatened use of a dangerous weapon, explosives, or fire, shall be fined under this title or imprisoned not more than ten years, or both; and if death results from the acts committed in violation of this section or if such acts include kidnapping or an attempt to kidnap, aggravated sexual abuse, or an attempt to commit aggravated sexual abuse, or an attempt to kill, shall be fined under this title, or imprisoned for any term of years or for life, or both, or may be sentenced to death.

51. Johns, at 520.

52. Gross et. al., at 102.

53. *Id.* at 120.

54. *Id.*

55. *Id.*

56. *Id.*

57. *Id.*

58. *Id.*

59. *Id.* at 102.

60. Keenan et al., at 218.

61. *Id.*

62. Jared Bennet, *Kentucky Jails Made $9.6 Million off Jail Communication in FY2020*, WFPL, July 15, 2021, https://wfpl.org/kycir-kentucky-jails-made-9-6-million-off-jail-communication-in-fy2020/.

63. Education data was collected by the US Census Bureau and covers public school children prekindergarten through twelfth grade. Prison data from the Vera Institute was collected in each state using a department of corrections survey. Corrections departments from forty states completed and returned the survey, which asked respondents to provide prison expenditures paid by the department of corrections, as well as prison costs paid by other agencies. CNN, *Education vs. Prison Costs,* https://money.cnn.com/infographic/economy/education-vs-prison-costs/.

64. *Id.*

65. Sean Bryant, *The Business Model of Private Prisons,* INVESTOPEDIA, June 21, 2021, https://www.investopedia.com/articles/investing/062215/business-model-private-prisons.asp.

66. *Id.*

67. *Id.*

68. *Id.*

69. *Id.*

70. No Kickbacks Campaign, https://paroleillinois.org/2021/06/21/no-kickbacks-campaign/.

71. Lisa Valder, *Local Spending on Jails Tops $25 Billion in Latest Nationwide Data,* PEW, Jan. 29, 2021, https://www.pewtrusts.org/en/research-and-analysis/issue-briefs/2021/01/local-spending-on-jails-tops-$25-billion-in-latest-nationwide-data.

72. *Id.*

73. *Id.*

74. Aaron Littman, *Jails, Sheriffs, and Carceral Policymaking,* 74 VAND. L. REV. 861 (2021).

75. *Id.*

76. *Id.*

77. *Id.*

78. *Id.*

CHAPTER 5

1. The Antiterrorism and Effective Death Penalty Act of 1996, Pub. L. No. 104-132, 110 Stat. 1214 is a major mid-1990s reform of habeas corpus as used to challenge criminal convictions. It was signed into law on April 24, 1996, by President Bill Clinton. It was introduced after the 1993 World Trade Center bombing and the 1995 Oklahoma City bombing. Among other provisions, procedurally, AEDPA bans successive petitions by the same person, requiring defendants to put all their claims into one appeal. Substantively, it narrows the

grounds on which successful habeas claims can be made, allowing claims only to succeed when the convictions were contrary to "clearly established federal law" or an "unreasonable determination of the facts in light of the evidence." *State Custody; Remedies in Federal Courts*, 28 U.S.C. § 2254; Lee Kovarsky, *AEDPA's Wrecks: Comity, Finality, and Federalism*, 82 Tul. L. Rev. 443 (2007), https://www.law.cornell.edu/wex/antiterrorism_and_effective_death _penalty_act_of_1996_(aedpa).

2. Pamela Bucy Pierson, *RICO Trends: From Gangsters to Class Actions*, 65 S. C. L. Rev. 213, 216 (2013).

3. *Id.*

4. *Id.*

5. *Id.*

6. *Id.* at 217.

7. *Id.*

8. *Id.*

9. *Id.*

10. *Id.* See also Racketeer Influenced and Corrupt Organizations, 18 U.S.C.S. § 1961.

11. Natalie Y. Moore & Lance Williams, The Almighty Black P Stone Nation: The Rise, Fall, and Resurgence of an American Gang (2011): "Congress had enacted *RICO* in 1970 to fight organized crime and the mob. Officials realized that they could use the law beyond that scope, and in the 1980s street *gangs* increasingly saw *RICO* charges leveled against members."

12. M. G. Shein, *Racial Disparity in Crack Cocaine Sentencing*, Crim. Just., 8, 28 (1993).

13. Blakely v. Washington, 124 S. Ct. 2531 (2004).

14. Apprendi v. New Jersey, 530 U.S. 466 (2000).

15. United States v. Booker, 125 S. Ct. 738, 756 (2005).

16. *Id.* at 751.

17. *Id.* at 756.

18. *Id.* at 756.

19. *Id.* at 757.

20. United States v. Bass, 266 F.3d 532 (6th Cir. 2001).

21. Rory K. Little, *The Federal Death Penalty: History and Some Thoughts about the Department of Justice's Role*, 26 Fordham Urban. L.J., 347, 478 (1999), referencing court-ordered discovery revealing that "of 296 defendants submitted for capital case review between January 27, 1995, and August 10, 1998, 55% were African-American and 80% were non-white. . . . [A]mong the eighty-one defendants actually authorized for death penalty prosecution: 57% were African-American and 72% were non-white" (citations omitted); see also David Bruck et al., *Federal Death Penalty Prosecutions: 1988–1999* (last modified Aug. 9, 1999), http://www.capdefnet.org/2_summ_cases_ auth_frames.htm.

22. STATISTICAL ABSTRACT OF THE UNITED STATES: 1998 §1 (Population) Table No. 18.

23. *Sourcebook of Criminal Justice Statistics Online*: 1997 Table 6.43, www.albany.edu/sourcebook /1995/pdf/t643.pdf.

24. *Id.*

25. Little, at 478.

26. See generally Village of Arlington Heights v. Metropolitan Housing Development Corp., 429 U.S. 252. See also David Crump, *Evidence, Race, Intent and Evil: The Paradox of Purposelessness in the Constitutional Race Discrimination Cases*, 27 HOFSTRA L. REV. 285 (Winter 1998); John Eisenberg et al., *Post-McCleskey Racial Discrimination Claims in Capital Cases*, 83 CORNELL L. REV. 1771.

27. Wayte v. United States, 470 U.S. 598 (1984).

28. *Id.* at 609 (footnote omitted).

29. United States v. Armstrong, 517 U.S. 456 (1996).

30. Marc Lacey & Raymond Bonner, *Reno Troubled by Death Penalty Statistics*, N. Y. TIMES, Sept. 13, 2000, https://www.nytimes.com/2000/09/13/us /reno-troubled-by-death-penalty-statistics.html.

31. *Id.*

32. The order told the government to turn over: (a) a complete list of all cases since 1995 in which the federal government has charged crimes under the Anti-Drug Abuse Statute, 21 U.S.C. § 848, including a breakdown by state, district, and office; (b) a list of the race, religion, and ethnic background of each of these charged defendants; (c) the name of each United States Attorney to handle each of these aforementioned cases; (d) a list of which of these aforementioned cases was recommended to the Attorney General as a death penalty case; (e) the race, religion, and ethnic background of each defendant whose case was recommended to the Attorney General as being a death penalty case; (f) a complete list of which of these were authorized as death penalty cases by the Attorney General's office; (g) a complete list of which of these defendants entered into plea bargains, were found guilty and either sentenced to death or sentenced to less, were acquitted; (h) a complete list of the race, religion, and ethnic background of these defendants.

33. *Federal Rules of Civil Procedure*, FRCRP 16(d)(1).

34. United States v. Bass, 266 F. 3d 532 (6th Cir. 2001).

35. United States v. Bass, 536 U.S. 862, 862–63 (2002).

CHAPTER 6

1. Callins v. Collins, 510 U.S. 1141, 1145 (1994); Justice Blackmun:

From this day forward, I no longer shall tinker with the machinery of death. For more than 20 years I have endeavored—indeed, I have struggled—along with a majority of this Court, to develop procedural and substantive rules that would lend more than the mere appearance of fairness to the death penalty endeavor. 1 [****11] Rather than continue to coddle the Court's delusion that the desired level of fairness has been achieved and the need for regulation eviscerated, I feel [****10] morally and intellectually obligated simply to concede that the death penalty experiment has failed. It is virtually self-evident to me now that no combination of procedural rules or substantive regulations ever can save the death penalty from its inherent constitutional deficiencies. The basic question—does the system accurately and consistently determine which defendants "deserve" to die?—cannot be answered in the affirmative.

2. The National Association for Public Defense, the National Association of Criminal Defense Lawyers, the National Legal Aid and Defender Association, the ACLU, the Brennan Center, the Sixth Amendment Center, and the American Constitution Society.

3. CJ Griffin, Christine Filip, Cynthia Roseberry, David Miller, David Carroll, Derwyn Bunton, Ernie Lewis, Evan Griffith, Geoff Burkhart, Jo-Ann Wallace, Jeff Sherr, Jon Rapping, Joseph Russo, Kevin Roberts, Kylleen Tremont, Lori James-Townes, Maha Jweied, Michael Mrozinski, Raymond M. Brown, Sam Dennis, Joni Stahlman, Stephen Hanlon, Sara Totonchi, Tony Thedford, Twyla Carter, E. Kate Cohn, and many others as well.

References

ABA MODEL RULES OF PROF'L CONDUCT R. 3.8(f). (2013).

ABA STANDING COMM. ON PRO. REGUL. OF THE AM. BAR ASS'N CTR. FOR PRO. RESP., 2017 SURVEY ON LAWYER DISCIPLINE SYSTEMS (2019), http://www.american bar.org/content/dam/aba/administrative/professional_responsibility/2017 sold-results.pdf [https://perma.cc/ER4Q-VDEM].

MICHELLE ALEXANDER, THE NEW JIM CROW: MASS INCARCERATION IN THE AGE OF COLORBLINDNESS (2010).

Jennifer M. Allen, *Free for All a Free for All: The Supreme Court's Abdication of Duty in Failing to Establish Standards for Indigent Defense*, 27 LAW & INEQ. 365 (Summer 2009).

Antiterrorism and Effective Death Penalty Act, 104, 110 Stat. at 1219.

AP, *Cops Bought Burger King for Dylann Roof Following His Arrest*, ABC NEWS, June 23, 2015, https://abc7.com/dylann-roof-south-carolina-church -shooting-emanuel-african-methodist-episcopal/801013/.

Apprendi v. New Jersey, 530 U.S. 466 (2000).

Atkins v. Virginia, 536 U.S. 304 (2002).

The Bail Project, *After Cash Bail: A Framework for Reimagining Pretrial Justice*, https://bailproject.org/after-cash-bail/.

Batson v. Kentucky, 476 U.S. 79, 82 (1986).

Lara A. Bazelon, *Hard Lessons: The Role of Law Schools in Addressing Prosecutorial Misconduct*, 16 BERKELEY J. CRIM. L. 391, 411 (2011).

BBC, *Central Park Five: The True Story behind When They See Us*, BBC NEWS, June 12, 2019, https://www.bbc.com/news/newsbeat-48609693.

Sara Sun Beale, *The News Media's Influence on Criminal Justice Policy: How Market-driven News Promotes Punitiveness*, 48 WM. & MARY L. REV. 397, 459 (2006).

Jared Bennet, *Kentucky Jails Made $9.6 Million off Jail Communication in FY2020*, WFPL, July 15, 2021, https://wfpl.org/kycir-kentucky-jails-made -9-6-million-off-jail-communication-in-fy2020/.

Tanja Rapus Benton et al., *Eyewitness Memory Is Still Not Common Sense: Comparing Jurors, Judges and Law Enforcement to Eyewitness Experts*, 20.1 APP. COG. PSYCH.: THE OFF. J. OF THE SOC. FOR APP. RES. IN MEM. AND COG. 115–29 (2006).

Dr. Shari R. Berkowitz, *Expert Report Prepared for People v. Luna* (No. 10-CF-4004).

Better Government Association, *The High Cost of Wrongful Convictions*, BETTER GOVT ASSOC., http://www.bettergov.org/investigations/wrongful _convictions_1.aspx.

Blakely v. Washington, 124 S. Ct. 2531 (2004).

Brady v. Maryland, 373 U.S. 83, 87 (1963).

David Bruck et al., Federal Death Penalty Prosecutions 1988–1999 (last modified Aug 9., 1999), http://www.capdefnet.org/2_summ_cases_ auth_frames .htm.

Sean Bryant, *The Business Model of Private Prisons*, INVESTOPEDIA, June 21, 2021, https://www.investopedia.com/articles/investing/062215/business -model-private-prisons.asp.

Curtis Bunn, *10 Slave Codes That Were Designed to Oppress and Humiliate Black People*, ATLANTA BLACK STAR (Dec. 22, 2014), https://atlantablackstar .com/2014/12/22/10-slave-codes-that-were-designed-to-oppress-and-humil iate-black-people/.

Alafair S. Burke, *Prosecutorial Agnosticism*, 8 OHIO ST. J. CRIM. L. 79 (2010).

California Innocence Project, *False Testimony/Confessions*, https://california innocenceproject.org/issues-we-face/false-confessions/#:~:text=One%20 of%20the%20most%20well,pressure%20to%20find%20those%20respon sible.

California v. Hodari D., 499 U.S. 621, 623 n.1 (1991).

Callins v. Collins, 510 U.S. 1141, 1145 (1994).

Jeremy L. Carlson, *The Professional Duty of Prosecutors to Disclose Exculpatory Evidence to the Defense: Implications of Rule 3.8(D) of the Model Rules of Professional Conduct*, 28 J. LEGAL PRO. 125, 126 (2004).

Mia Carpiniello, *Striking a Sincere Balance: A Reasonable Black Person Standard For "Location Plus Evasion" Terry Stops*, 6 MICH. J. RACE & L. 355, 357–70 (2001).

Sanjay Chhablani, *Disentangling the Sixth Amendment*, 11 U. PA. J. CONST. L. 487, 492 (2009).

The Civil Rights Bill of 1866, HISTORY, ART, & ARCHIVES UNITED STATES HOUSE OF REPRESENTATIVES, https://history.house.gov/Historical-High lights/1851-1900/The-Civil-Rights-Bill-of-1866/.

CNN, *Education vs. Prison Costs*, https://money.cnn.com/infographic/economy /education-vs-prison-costs/.

Kate Cohn, *When the Home Team Calls Their Own Balls and Strikes: The Problem of Brady Violations, Accountability, and Making the Case for a Washington State Commission on Prosecutorial Conduct*, 19 SEATTLE J. FOR SOC. JUST 161 (2020).

Coleman v. Commonwealth, 226 Va. 31 (1983).

Coleman v. Thompson, 501 U.S. 722 (1991).

Paul Colomy, *Making Youth Violence Visible: The News Media and the Summer of Violence*, 77 Denv. U. L. REV. 661, 672–73 (2000).

Commonwealth v. Walker, 625 Pa. 450, 92 A.3d 766, 782–83 (Pa. 2014).

Laura Connelly, *Cross-Racial Identifications: Solutions to the "They All Look Alike" Effect*, 21 MICH. J. RACE & L. 125 (2015). https://repository.law .umich.edu/cgi/viewcontent.cgi?article=1052&context=mjrl.

Connick v. Thompson, 563 U.S. 51 (2011).

Crisp v. Duckworth, 743 F.2d 580, 584 (7th Cir. 1984).

David Crump, *Evidence, Race, Intent and Evil: The Paradox of Purposelessness in the Constitutional Race Discrimination Cases*, 27 HOFSTRA L. REV. 285 (Winter 1998).

Kenneth A. Deffenbacher & Elizabeth F. Loftus, *Do Jurors Share a Common Understanding Concerning Eyewitness Behavior?* 6.1 LAW AND HUM. BEHAV. 15–30 (1982).

Deprivation of Rights Under Color of Law, 18 U.S.C. § 242 (1996).

JIM DWYER, PETER J. NEUFELD, & BARRY SCHECK, ACTUAL INNOCENCE: FIVE DAYS TO EXECUTION AND OTHER DISPATCHES FROM THE WRONGLY CONVICTED, (2000).

Edmonson v. Leesville Concrete Co., 500 U.S. 614, 633–34 (1991).

John Eisenberg et al., *Post-McCleskey Racial Discrimination Claims in Capital Cases*, 83 CORNELL L. REV. 1771.

Daniel Epps & William Ortman, *The Defender General*, 168 U. PA. L. REV. 1469 (2020).

Sarah Eschholz, *Crime on Television: Issues in Criminal Justice*, 9 J. INST. JUST. INT'L STUD. 9, 9–11 (2003).

Faretta v. California, 422 U.S. 806 (1975).

Federal Rules of Civil Procedure, FRCRP 16(d)(1).

FindLaw, *What Is Prosecutorial Discretion?*, https://www.findlaw.com /criminal/criminal-procedure/what-is-prosecutorial-discretion-.html #:~:text=Prosecutorial%20discretion%20is%20when%20a,which%20criminal%20charges%20to%20file.

Richard K. Gabriel, *Values, Beliefs, and Demographics in Selecting Jurors*, ATLA-CLE 49 (Winter 2002).

BRANDON GARRETT, CONVICTING THE INNOCENT (2011).

Adam M. Gershowitz, *Prosecutorial Shaming: Naming Attorneys to Reduce Prosecutorial Misconduct*, 42 U.C. DAVIS L. REV. 1059, 1075 (2008).

Gideon v. Wainwright, 372 U.S. 335 (1963).

Glasser v. United States, 315 U.S. 60 (1942).

Joseph Goldstein, *Teenager Claims Body-Cams Show the Police Framed Him. What Do You See?* N. Y. TIMES, November 19, 2018, https://www.nytimes .com/2018/11/19/nyregion/body-cameras-police-marijuana-arrest.html.

Robert Granfield & Thomas Koenig, *It's Hard to Be a Human Being and a Lawyer: Young Attorneys and the Confrontation with Ethical Ambiguity in Legal Practice*, 105 W. VA. L. REV. 495, 502 (2003).

Griffith v. Slinkard, 44 N.E. 1001, 1002 (1896).

SAMUEL R. GROSS, MAURICE J. POSSLEY, KAITLIN JACKSON ROLL & KLARA HUBER STEPHENS, GOVERNMENT MISCONDUCT AND CONVICTING THE INNOCENT: THE ROLE OF PROSECUTORS, POLICE AND OTHER LAW ENFORCEMENT 76 (2020), https:// www.law.umich.edu/special/exoneration/Documents/Government_Miscon duct_and_Convicting_the_Innocent.pdf [https://perma.cc/Q333-3GWY] at 102.

Aya Gruber, *Victim Wrongs: The Case for a General Criminal Defense Based on Wrongful Victim Behavior in an Era of Victims' Rights*, 76 TEMP. L. REV. 645 (2003).

David Harris, *The Appearance of Justice: Court TV, Conventional Television, and Public Understanding of the Criminal Justice System*, 35 ARIZ. L. REV. 785, 809 (1993).

Erica J. Hashimoto, *Resurrecting Autonomy: The Criminal Defendant's Right to Control the Case*, 90 B.U. L. REV. 1147, 1164 (2010).

History.com Editors, *Black Codes*, HISTORY, https://www.history.com/topics /black-history/black-codes.

Imbler v. Pachtman, 424 U.S. 409, 422–23 (1976).

Innocence Project, www.innocenceproject.org.

In Re Gault, 387 U.S. 1 (1967).

Johnson v. Zerbst, 304 U.S. 458 (1938).

Margaret Z. Johns, *Unsupportable and Unjustified: A Critique of Absolute Prosecutorial Immunity*, 80 FORDHAM L. REV. 509, 510 (2011).

Rick Jones, Gerald B. Lefcourt, Barry J. Pollack, Norman L. Reimer, & Kyle O'Dowd, *The Trial Penalty: The Sixth Amendment Right to Trial on the Verge of Extinction and How to Save It*, National Association of Criminal Defense Lawyers, 4–5, 2018, https://www.nacdl.org/getattachment/95b7f0f5-90df -4f9f-9115-520b3f58036a/the-trial-penalty-the-sixth-amendment-right-to -trial-on-the-verge-of-extinction-and-how-to-save-it.pdf.

David Keenan, et al., *Myth of Prosecutorial Accountability after* Connick v. Thompson*: Why Existing Professional Responsibility Measures Cannot Protect against Prosecutorial Misconduct*, 121 YALE L.J. F. 203, 214 (2012).

Lee Kovarsky, *AEDPA's Wrecks: Comity, Finality, and Federalism*, 82 TUL. L. REV. 443 (2007), https://www.law.cornell.edu/wex/antiterrorism_and_effec tive_death_penalty_act_of_1996_(aedpa).

Jason Kreag, *Disclosing Prosecutorial Misconduct*, 72 Vand. L. Rev. 297, 305–306 (2019).

Ku Klux Klan Act of 1871, ch. 22, 17 Stat. 13 (1871) (codified at 42 U.S.C. § 1983), https://www.law.cornell.edu/uscode/text/42/1983.

Kyles v. Whitley, 514 U.S. 419 (1995).

Marc Lacey & Raymond Bonner, *Reno Troubled by Death Penalty Statistics*, N. Y. Times, Sept. 13, 2000, https://www.nytimes.com/2000/09/13/us/reno -troubled-by-death-penalty-statistics.html.

Alan K. Lamm, *Slave Codes*, NCPEDIA (2006), https://www.ncpedia.org /slave-codes.

Cara Laney & Elizabeth Loftus, *Emotional Content of True and False Memories*, 16 Memory, 500–16 (2008).

Cynthia Kwei Yung Lee, *Race and Self-Defense: Towards a Normative Conception of Reasonableness*, 81 Minn. L. Rev. 367, 455–70 (1996).

Wanda M. L. Lee, Cross Culturing Counseling (1999).

Richard A. Leo & Brittany Liu, *What Do Potential Jurors Know about Police Interrogation Techniques and False Confessions*, 27 Behav. Sci. & L. 381 (2009).

Linda J. Levine & David A. Pizarro, *Emotion and Memory Research: A Grumpy Overview*, 22 Social Cognition, 530–54 (2005).

Ernest F. Lidge III, *Perp Walks and Prosecutioral Ethics*, 7 Nev. L. J. 55 (2006–2007).

Rory K. Little, *The Federal Death Penalty: History and Some Thoughts about the Department of Justice's Role*, 26 Fordham Urban. L.J., 347, 478 (1999).

Aaron Littman, *Jails, Sheriffs, and Carceral Policymaking*, 74 Vand. L. Rev. 861 (2021).

Elizabeth F. Loftus, Eyewitness Testimony, 1979.

Elizabeth Loftus, *How Reliable Is Your Memory*, TED (2013), http://www.ted .com/talks/elizabeth_loftus_the_fiction_of_memory.html.

Elizabeth Loftus & Katherine Ketcham, Witness for the Defense: The Accused, the Eyewitness, and the Expert who puts Memory on Trial (1991).

Katesha Long, *Debunking the Broken Windows Theory in Policing: An Incident and Badge of Slavery*, 4 How. Hum. & Civ. Rts. L. REV. 77 (2020).

Lauren Sudeall Lucas, *Effectively Ineffective: The Failure of Courts to Address Underfunded Indigent Defense Systems*. Harv. L. Rev., 118, 1731 (2004).

Andrea D. Lyon, Angel of Death Row: My Life as a Death Penalty Defense Lawyer, chs. 4 & 5 (2010).

Andrea D. Lyon et. al. Post-Conviction Practice: A Manual for Illinois Attorneys, Illinois State Bar Association, (2012).

Andrea D. Lyon & Mort Smith, Team Defense in Criminal Cases (2014).

Manson v. Brathwaite, 432 U.S. 98 (1977).

BOB MARLEY AND THE WAILERS, *War*, on RASTAMAN VIBRATION (Island Records 1976).

McCleskey v. Kemp, 481 U.S. 279 (1987).

McFarland v. State, 928 S.W.2d 482 (Tex. Crim. App. 1996) (per curiam), reh'g denied, 928 S.W.2d 482 (Tex. Crim. App. 1996), cert. denied sub nom. McFarland v. Texas, 519 U.S. 1119 (1997).

Connie McNeely, *Perceptions of the Criminal Justice System: Television Imagery and Public Knowledge in the United States*, 1 J. OF CRIM. JUST. AND POPULAR CULTURE, 3–5, 10 (1995).

Miller v. Alabama, 567 U.S. 460 (2012).

Miranda v. Arizona, 384 U.S. 436 (1966).

Missouri v. Frye, 566 U.S. 133, 144 (2012).

NATALIE Y. MOORE & LANCE WILLIAMS, THE ALMIGHTY BLACK P STONE NATION: THE RISE, FALL, AND RESURGENCE OF AN AMERICAN GANG (2001).

Morgan v. Illinois, 504 U.S. 719 (1992).

Morris v. Slappy, 461 U.S. 1 (1983).

NAT'L ARCHIVES, FED. REG., ANN. DETERMINATION OF AVERAGE COST OF INCARCERATION FEE (COIF) (2019), https://www.federalregister.gov/documents/2019/11/19/2019-24942/annual-determination-of-average-cost-of-incarceration-fee-coif [https://perma.cc/RS3J-V883].

National Registry of Exonerations, *Exonerations by Year, DNA and Non-DNA*, https://www.law.umich.edu/special/exoneration/Pages/Exoneration-by-Year.aspx.

National Registry of Exonerations, *False Confessions*, https://www.law.umich.edu/special/exoneration/Pages/False-Confessions.aspx.

Nadra Kareem Nittle, *The Black Codes and Why They Still Matter Today*, THOUGHT CO., https://www.thoughtco.com/the-black-codes-4125744.

No Kickbacks Campaign, https://paroleillinois.org/2021/06/21/no-kickbacks-campaign/.

Anna Offit, *Prosecuting in the Shadow of the Jury*, 113 NW. U. L. REV. 1071, 1083 (2019).

William Ortman, *Second-Best Criminal Justice*, 96 WASH. U.L. REV. 1061, 1066 (2019).

Timothy P. O'Toole & Giovanna Shay, *Manson v. Brathwaite Revisited: Towards a New Rule of Decision for Due Process Challenges to Eyewitness Identification Procedures*, 41 VAL. U.L. REV. 112–13 (Fall 2006).

People v. Lerma, 2016 IL 118496, ¶¶ 24–25, 47 N.E.3d 985.

People v. Randall, 283 Ill. App. 3d 1019, 1026, 671 N.E.2d 60, 66 (1st Dist. 1996).

People v. Whitehead, 169 Ill 2d 355, 375 (1996).

Pamela Bucy Pierson, *RICO Trends: From Gangsters to Class Actions*, 65 S. C. L. REV. 213, 216 (2013).

Kimberlianne Podlas, *As Seen on TV: the Normative Influence of Syndi-court on Contemporary Litigiousness*, 11 Vill. Sports & Ent. L.J. 1, 19–23 (2004).

Powell v. Alabama, 287 U.S. 45, 53 (1932).

Eyal Press, *A Fight To Expose the Hidden Human Costs of Incarceration*, The New Yorker, Aug. 16, 2021, https://www.newyorker.com/magazine /2021/08/23/a-fight-to-expose-the-hidden-human-costs-of-incarceration.

Roger Przybylski, et al., Trends and Issues, 1997: Illinois Criminal Justice Information Authority 77 (1997).

Public Act 099-0258; 705 ILCS 405/5-130.

Jeffrey J. Rachlinski et al., *Does Unconscious Racial Bias Affect Trial Judges?* 84 Notre L. Rev. 1195, 1196 (2009).

Racketeer Influenced and Corrupt Organizations, 18 U.S.C.S. § 1961.

Jonathan Rapping, Gideon's Promise: A Public Defender Movement to Transform Criminal Justice, (2020).

L. Song Richardson, *Arrest Efficiency and the Fourth Amendment*, 95 Minn. L. Rev. 2035, 2044 (2011).

Dorothy Roberts, *The Social and Moral Cost of Mass Incarceration in African American Communities*. 56 Stan. L. Rev., 1271 (2003).

Roper v. Simmons, 543 U.S. 551 (2005).

Benjamin Rosenberg, *Rethinking the Right to Due Process in Connection with Pre-trial Identification Procedures: An Analysis and a Proposal*, 79 Ky. L.J. 259, 260 (1990/1991).

Scott Sayare et al., *French Shocked by I.M.F. Chief's "Perp Walk,"* N. Y. Times, May 16, 2011, http://thelede.blogs.nytimes.com/2011/05/16/french -shocked-by-i-m-f-chiefs-perp-walk/.

Samson J. Schatz, *Interrogated with Intellectual Disabilities: The Risks of False Confession*, 70 Stan. L. Rev. 643, 651 (2018).

R. S. Schmechel et al. *Beyond the Ken? Testing Jurors' Understanding of Eye-witness Reliability Evidence*, 46 Jurimetrics 177 (2006).

Sentencing Project, *State by State Data*, https://www.sentencingproject.org /the-facts/#map?dataset-option=SIR.

M. G. Shein, *Racial Disparity in Crack Cocaine Sentencing*, Crim. Just., 8, 28 (1993).

Daniel J. Simons & Christopher F. Chabris, *What People Believe about How Memory Works: A Representative Survey of the US Population*, 6.8 PLoS One (2011).

Catherine Smith, *Unconscious Bias and "Outsider" Interest Convergence*, 40 Conn. L. Rev. 1077, 1086 (2008).

Juliet Sorenson, *Ten Years Ago Illinois Abolished the Death Penalty. These People Helped Make it Happen*, Injustice Watch, May 7, 2021, https:// www.injusticewatch.org/commentary/2021/illinois-death-penalty-abolition/.

Sourcebook of Criminal Justice Statistics Online: 1997 Table 6.43 www .albany.edu/sourcebook/1995/pdf/t643.pdf.

State Custody; Remedies in Federal Courts, 28 U.S.C. § 2254.

State v. Guilbert, 306 Conn. 218, 49 A.3d 705, 723–24 (Conn. 2012).

State v. Dubose, 2005 WI 126, 285 Wis. 2d 143, 699 N.W.2d 582, 591–92 (Wis. 2005).

STATISTICAL ABSTRACT OF THE UNITED STATES: 1998 §1 (Population) Table No. 18.

Laurence Steinberg & Elizabeth Scott, *Less Guilty by Reason of Adolescence: Developmental Immaturity, Diminished Responsibility, and the Juvenile Death Penalty*, 58 AM. PSYCH. 1009, 1014 (2003).

Russell Stetler, *Mental Health Evidence and the Capital Defense Function: Prevailing Norms*, 82 UMKC L. REV. 407 (2014).

BRYAN STEVENSON, JUST MERCY: A STORY OF JUSTICE AND REDEMPTION (2014).

Megan T. Stevenson, *Distortion of Justice: How the Inability to Pay Bail Affects Case Outcomes*, 34 J. OF L., ECON., & ORG 511–42 (2018).

Strickland v. Washington, 466 U.S. 668 (1984).

Thomas P. Sullivan & Maurice Possley, *The Chronic Failure to Discipline Prosecutors for Misconduct: Proposals for Reform*, 105 J. CRIM. L. & CRIMINOLOGY 881, 923 (2015).

DR. SUNWOLF, PRACTICAL JURY DYNAMICS: FROM ONE JUROR'S TRIAL PERCEPTIONS TO THE GROUPS'S DECISION-MAKING PROCESS (2004).

Ray Surette, *The Media, the Public and Criminal Justice Policy*, 2 J. INST. JUST. INT'L STUD. 39, 43 (2003).

Jennifer M. Talarico & David C. Rubin, *Confidence, Not Consistency, Characterizes Flashbulb Memories*, 14 PSYCH. SCI, 455–61 (2003).

JENNIFER THOMPSON-CANNINO, RONALD COTTON, & ERIN TORNEO, PICKING COTTON: OUR MEMOIR OF INJUSTICE AND REDEMPTION (2009).

Roberto Tijerina, *Black Codes, Jim Crow, and Social Control in the South*, STMU HISTORY MEDIA (Mar. 22, 2017), https://www.stmuhistorymedia.org /the-south-and-vigilante-justice/.

U.S. Const. amend. VI.

U.S. Const. amend. XIV, § 1.

United States Dept. of Justice, *Justice Manual, Title 9, Criminal, Capital Crimes*, https://www.justice.gov/jm/jm-9-10000-capital-crimes.

U.S. DEP'T OF JUST., OFF. OF SOLIC. GEN., SOLIC. GEN. FREDERICK WILLIAM LEHMANN (2019), https://www.justice.gov/osg/bio/frederick-w-lehmann [https:// perma.cc/KHC2-6VH9].

United States ex rel. Griffith v. Hulick, 587 F. Supp. 2d 899, 902 (N.D. Ill. 2008).

United States v. Agurs, 427 U.S. 97 (1976).

United States v. Armstrong, 517 U.S. 456 (1996).

United States v. Bagley, 473 U.S. 667 (1985).

United States v. Bass, 266 F.3d 532 (6th Cir. 2001).

United States v. Bass, 536 U.S. 862, 862–63 (2002).

United States v. Booker, 125 S. Ct. 738, 756 (2005).

United States v. Cronic, 466 U.S. at 657 (1984).

United States v. Wade, 388 U.S. 218, 228 (1967).

Lisa Valder, *Local Spending on Jails Tops $25 Billion in Latest Nationwide Data*, PEW, Jan. 29, 2021, https://www.pewtrusts.org/en/research-and-analy sis/issue-briefs/2021/01/local-spending-on-jails-tops-$25-billion-in-latest -nationwide-data.

Village of Arlington Heights v. Metropolitan Housing Development Corp., 429 U.S. 252.

Wainwright v. Sykes, 433 U.S. 72, 87 (1977).

Adam Walinsky, *What It's Like to Be in Hell*, N. Y. TIMES, Dec. 4, 1987, https:// www.nytimes.com/1987/12/04/opinion/what-it-s-like-to-be-in-hell.html.

Wayte v. United States, 470 U.S. 598 (1984).

Henry Weinstein, *Inmate in Texas Sleeping-Lawyer Case Pleads Guilty*, L.A. TIMES, June 20, 2003, https://www.latimes.com/archives/la-xpm-2003-jun -20-na-sleep20-story.html.

Debra Cassens Weiss, *Contract Public Defenders in this State Make About $5 per Hour after Overhead, New Study Says*, ABA J., July 9, 2020, https:// www.abajournal.com/news/article/contract-public-defenders-in-this-state -make-about-5-an-hour-after-overhead-study-says.

Debra Cassens Weiss, *Sleeping Lead Lawyer Doesn't Justify Overturning Capital Conviction, Federal Judge Rules*, ABA J., April 10, 2019, https://www .abajournal.com/news/article/sleeping-lead-lawyer-doesnt-justify-overturn ing-capital-conviction-federal-judge-rules.

Wheat v. United States, 486 U.S. 153 (1988).

Christopher Wills, *Illinois Death Penalty Abolished: Pat Quinn Signs Death Penalty Ban, Clears Death Row*, HUFFINGTON POST, Mar. 9, 2011, http:// www.huffingtonpost.com/2011/03/08/illinois-death-penalty-ab_n_833250 .html.

Michael Wines, *Prosecutors Had the Wrong Man. They Prosecuted Him Anyway*, N. Y. TIMES, January 17, 2018, https://www.nytimes.com /2018/01/17/us/prosecutors-new-orleans-evidence.html.

Richard A Wise et al., *What US Law Enforcement Officers Know and Believe About Eyewitness Factors, Eyewitness Interviews and Identification Procedures*, 25.3 APP. COG. PSYCH. 488–500 (2011).

Richard Wise et al., *What US Prosecutors and Defence Attorneys Know and Believe about Eyewitness Testimony*, 23.9 APP. COG. PSYCH.: THE OFF. J. OF THE SOC. FOR APP. RES. IN MEM. AND COG, 1266–1281 (2009).

Deputy Attorney General Sally Q. Yates, *Eyewitness Identification: Procedures for Conducting Photo Arrays: Memorandum for Heads of Department Law Enforcement Components All Department Prosecutors* (Jan. 6, 2017), https://www.justice.gov/file/923201/download.

Emily Yoffe, *Innocence Is Irrelevant*, THE ATLANTIC, September 2017, https://www.theatlantic.com/magazine/archive/2017/09/innocence-is-irrelevant/534171/.

Kimberly Helene Zelnick, *In Gideon's Shadow: The Loss of Defendant Autonomy and the Growing Scope of Attorney Discretion,* 30 AM. J. CRIM. L. 363, 373 (2003).

Index

About the Author

Andrea D. Lyon is a criminal defense attorney (the principal in the criminal defense firm Lyon Law), a death penalty expert, an author, a former professor and law school dean, and an occasional target of the "How can you represent those people?" blogosphere.

Andrea has tried more than 130 homicide cases, more than 30 of which were potential capital cases. Of those thirty clients, nineteen were convicted and found eligible for the death penalty. With the help of her team, Andrea prevented all nineteen clients from being sentenced to death.

When Andrea joined the Homicide Task Force of the Cook County, Illinois, Public Defenders' Office in 1979, only one other woman had served on the team—briefly. Not only did Andrea stick around, but two years later, she became the first woman in the nation to act as lead counsel on a death penalty case. Eventually, she was named chief of the Homicide Task Force, supervising the work of twenty-two attorneys.

Over her forty years of lawyering, Andrea has been involved in several high-profile cases, including former Illinois governor George Ryan.

Andrea's legal memoir, *Angel of Death Row: My Life as a Death Penalty Defense Lawyer*, published in 2010, received a starred review from Kirkus and was voted "Next Great Read" by the American Booksellers Association. *Angel of Death Row* chronicles her struggle to humanize clients in the face of a criminal justice system that gives enormous advantage to the prosecution and stacks the cards according to wealth, race, and social status.She has also published more than fifty law review and bar journal articles as well as other books, including most recently: *The Feminine Sixth: Women in Criminal Defense* (2018) and *The Death Penalty: What's Keeping It Alive* (Rowman & Little-field, 2015).

Among various professional leadership positions, Andrea has served as president of the Illinois Association of Criminal Defense Lawyers and cochair of the Death Penalty Committee of the National Association of Criminal Defense Lawyers.

Among many awards and honors, Andrea received the National Coalition to Abolish the Death Penalty's Outstanding Legal Service Award, the Illinois Association of Criminal Defense Lawyers Lifetime Achievement Award, the Clarence Darrow Award, the NLADA Reginald Heber Smith Award for being the best advocate for the poor in the country, the American Constitution Society's Abner Mikva Legal Legends Award, and Operation Push's Rev. Dr. Martin Luther King Jr. and President Lyndon B. Johnson Dream-Makers Award.

Complete listings of publications, leadership positions, and awards are in Andrea's résumé, available at www.andrealyon.com.

Andrea divides her time between Valparaiso, Indiana, and Chicago, and is married to Arnold Glass. She has two adult children, William Glass and Dr. Samantha Glass.